Counting Stars

Celebrity Licensing & Endorsements

Dedicated to my Dewey and my son
who inspire me to count stars

Table of Contents

Introduction

I don't think the world is sold
I'm just doing what we're told...
Said no more counting dollars,
we'll be counting stars

These lyrics to the popular OneRepublic song *Counting Stars*, written by Ryan Tedder, inspired the title to this book, as the phrase *counting stars* encapsulates the subject matter of this book: an historical, psychological and legal analysis of celebrity endorsements. But in contrast to the lyric, at least with regard to today's celebrities, society often finds itself not only "counting stars," but "counting dollars."   I am, of course, equating the idea of "counting stars" with the fascination American culture has with celebrities, and equating the idea of "counting dollars" with the reality that a celebrity can generate significant income exploiting that fascination.

The phenomenon of being a "star" or "celebrity" is generally considered a fairly modern concept, created by the Golden Era of Hollywood, and perpetuated over the years by the growth of mass media, the Internet, social media and the current pop culture-driven society. But rather, as we'll discover, the concept of envying the leader's position in life has been with humanity since the dawn of creation.

The psychological and genetic fascination that society has for celebrities not only creates a person's stardom but at the same time affords that celebrity tremendous powers to exploit themselves. This results in many opportunities for the celebrity to become exploited, not only by the celebrities themselves but by those who have a vested interest in the celebrities' revenues. For this reason, many celebrities become cynical, as if they are mere puppets being manipulated by their "handlers" who reinforce the old adage that "the show must go on" regardless of the toll on the celebrity. Tedder's lyrics can be interpreted as expressing this very frustration.

So ultimately, we live in a world where society not only counts the stars, but count the dollars as well. Fans place great value on the respect they have for their favorite celebrities, and that fact is not lost on the major players in the entertainment, advertising, marketing and licensing industries. In the legal world, we describe this power of exploitation the "right of publicity" and we call the exploitation of that right an endorsement or a license.

This book explores the history of using celebrities to promote products, the psychological process behind society's star gazing, the different ways to measure a celebrity's influence, and various methods of exploiting it through a legal process called licensing. In the chapters that follow, we will continue our examination of the various facets of celebrity endorsements and licensing. It is intended as a primer for entrepreneurs and start-ups who would like to seek out opportunities to grow their businesses, as well as young students or lawyers who need a crash course in celebrity endorsements and licensing opportunities. It will begin by examining why we respond to celebrity endorsements by looking at the psychology behind our desires to associate with the rich and famous. In the chapters that follow, those attributes of a celebrity's persona that are licensable will be explored, things such as brand, persona, image, signature, voice, trademark, characteristics and possessions. Nothing related to a celebrity is outside the potential realm of exploitation, regardless of whether the celebrity is still working, or deceased. This will necessitate a foray into laws and statutes that exist to enforce a living person's rights of privacy and publicity as well as the rights of deceased celebrity's estates to enforce their post-mortem rights. Since an endorsement campaign is only as good as the celebrity's popularity, the various means of measuring a celebrity's fame will be investigated. Finally, the various legal elements and concepts arising in the areas of endorsements and licensing will be summarized and explained. In a very real sense, this is a book about *counting stars*, as well as *counting dollars*.

An Historical Perspective

All cultures throughout history, without exception, idolize those individuals among the throngs who seem to stand out or rise above, whether it be because they perform heroic deeds, possess special talents, exhibit unique skill or aptitude, or display exceptional beauty or strength. Humans possess an innate desire to glorify individuals for these types of things, perhaps derived from our genetic need to follow the leader of the pack.

Aristotle recognized this propensity when he said "beauty is a greater recommendation than any letter of introduction." By this, he means that society tends to place more emphasis on the physical attractiveness of a person than they do on their reputation. In the world of fame and celebrity, contrary to the popular idiom, you can very often "judge a book by its cover." An astute celebrity can easily exploit this keen psychological, sociological, and societal interest, even curiosity, in the beautiful and famous for significant financial gain. They can license their fame in the form of their persona, their name, likeness, voice and other physical attributes. This is celebrity endorsement.

Using celebrity endorsements to promote a product or service is not a new phenomenon, even if we limit our scope to the United States. Al Jolson endorsed *Luckies* brand cigarettes in the

1920's, Ronald Reagan posed with a *Chesterfield* in his mouth in the 1940's, Bob Hope pitched *American Express* in the late 1950's, Joe

Namath slipped into *Hanes* pantyhose in the 1970's, and Bill Cosby spooned out *Jell-O* brand pudding in the 1980's. Celebrity sports icons, such as Michael Jordan, Roger Federer and Tiger Woods, frequently earn much more endorsement and licensing revenues than they do from the earnings they receive playing the very sports that made them celebrities.

A great deal of information can be gleaned about celebrity endorsements in the current climate by considering the world's fascination with the National Football League's Super Bowl. It is the modern equivalent of the Romans thronging into the Coliseum to watch their favorite Gladiators do battle. Every year, more Americans watch the NFL's seasonal finale between its league conferences than any other activity on television, even when compared to such socially relevant news events like major political debates or elections. In fact, there are usually more people who watch the Super Bowl than there are those who vote in any given presidential election.

A prime example is Super Bowl XLVIII between the Seattle Seahawks and the Denver Broncos, which ended with the largest point spread in the history of game, as the Seahawks

6

emphatically dashing Peyton Manning's hopes of a second title ring by a score of 43-8, a thirty-five-point difference! No Super Bowl before or since has even come close to that differential. Despite this painful spectacle, the number of people watching still averaged 111.3 million, peaking late in the game at 117, keeping the Super Bowl on the top of the list of most-watched shows.[1] Like the Romans drawn to the Coliseum, our society enjoys a good battle, and will turn up to watch even if it is grossly one-sided.

There is nothing like competition, or the potential for competition, to attract a crowd, but as 2014's Super Bowl Nielsen ratings illustrate, it is not just the actual game that people come to watch: just as often it is the fanfare associated with the game. In fact, several studies indicate that as many as 50% of the viewers who tune in to the Super Bowl every year do so simply to watch the advertisements. This is a fact that is certainly not lost on the many merchants who clamor to be associated with the Super Bowl, some of whom are willing to spend as much as $8 million on a 60-second spot to advertise during the game (in 2014).

And why not? As Robert Siltanen, founder of the Los Angeles-based advertising agency of Siltanen & Partners, points out in a online *Forbes* interview, "What other venue better assures that people are going to watch your commercial or talk about

---

[1] According to Nielsen Ratings.

your brand more than being on the Super Bowl?"[2] Combine this with the power of a celebrity's influence, and there is no quicker means to get people taking about your brand. For this reason, 2014's advertisements during the Super Bowl featured the likes of popular talk show host, Ellen DeGeneres, rock legend Bob Dylan, and actor turned ex-California governor turned actor, Arnold Schwarzenegger, all of whom, at least at that time, had significant influence on impressively large and loyal fan bases.

To reiterate, America is not the first culture to idolize and commercialize its celebrities, whether they be great competitors, actors, musicians, royalty, politicians, or mere citizens turned celebrity by exposure to wide audiences (like the myriad "reality television" celebrities created in American culture). As indicated earlier, long before the Declaration of Independence created an independent nation that was consumed with celebrity, the Romans exploited the more successful gladiators, many of whom were sought after commodities by the merchants who sold their wares in and around the Coliseum on the day of the big game, just as the advertisers today do in the Super Bowl commercials. We can only assume that the atmosphere around the Coliseum was similar to that surround the stadium on game day. The gladiators were offered compensation in exchange for their appearance on posters to place around the Coliseum (i.e., ancient billboards). The gladiators were paid to appear at the merchants' tables on

---

[2] Siltanen, Robert, "Yes, A Super Bowl Ad Really Is Worth $4 Million," Forbes.com, Jan. 29, 2014.

game day in hopes that their adoring fans would purchase more of their goods. Some academics may view this fame and fascination surrounding the gladiators of yore as somehow distinct from that surrounding modern celebrities like Peyton Manning, but the connection is undeniable. The fanfare surrounding the Coliseum is correctly seen as the earliest example of the same kind of commercialism that surrounds the Super Bowl. Both are examples of what we refer to today as "celebrity endorsements."

History shows that there is something in the human psyche that makes each of us desire a special connection to those unique few among us who rise to certain levels of fame and stardom. We want to be them: we want what they want and, given the choice, we like to use anything they might use to achieve their uniqueness, or form some special bond with them. "The reality is people want a piece of something they can't be," says Eli Portnoy, a branding strategist. "They live vicariously through the products and services [to which] those celebrities are tied...."[3] We'll explore the psychological basis of celebrity endorsements more specifically in the next chapter, but for now it is enough to understand that this phenomenon is the reason we respond so passionately to a celebrity endorsing a product or service.

---

[3] Creswell, Julie. "Nothing Sells Like Celebrity," *New York Times*, June 22, 2008.

Let's explore two other early examples of how advertisers use this phenomenon to increase the sales of their product and, in fact, change the course of history. In the late 1800's, a French

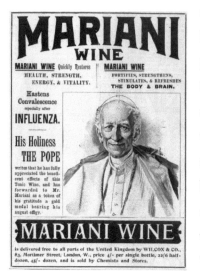

chemist named Angelo Mariani became intrigued with the properties of coca leaves. Mariani discovered that if he soaked the leaves in Bordeaux wine, the ethanol in the spirit extracted the cocaine, which bestowed additional "healing" qualities to the wine, creating a wonderful concoction he called "tonic."

Although the drink was ostensibly of high quality and very popular on that basis alone, its popularity did not truly explode until Pope Leo XIII awarded it the Vatican's highest honor, the gold medal. Local folklore was that the Pope carried a hip flask of the tonic with him everywhere he went. Soon after receiving the accolade of a "Gold Medal," Mariani also received permission to feature the image of none other than the Pope himself in advertisements for the wine.

But Mariani was not just content with associating the image with the product, his placards featured the actual *endorsement* of Pope Leo himself, who willingly extoled its virtues, touting that it would restore health, strength, energy and vitality. In legal circles, we often joke that a trial attorney can have no better witness than a "car full of nuns," so who better than the leader of the largest religious organization on the planet to extol the virtues of one's product?   Not surprisingly, the enhanced effects of "Vin Tonique Mariani" were soon world renowned and it was selling as fast as Mariani could make it. In the process, he had discovered another effective recipe: *fame+product=success.*

This recipe for exploiting the endorsement of a celebrity to increase product sales was not lost on other astute businessmen of the time. In Great Britain, J. S. Fry & Sons was a chocolate company started by Joseph Fry, a Quaker apothecary, in the mid 1700's. By 1884, the company, then owned by his progeny, could claim no less than seventeen prize medals and enjoyed a unique status as the manufacturers who supplied both the Queen and Prince of Wales with the delicious dark sweets.   Of course, the company was not shy about exploiting their special "royal warrant" in advertisements prominently featuring images of the very popular Queen Victoria.

As a result, the company grew into one of the largest and oldest chocolatiers in England, merging with a fellow Quaker-led company, Cadbury Chocolates, in the early 1900's. The Cadbury company can still lay claim to being a leader in the industry, as it was later acquired by Schweppes and then ultimately by its current owner, Kraft, in 2010. These two examples reinforce the principal in human behavior that the Romans discovered thousands of years before Fry or Mariani: *customers respond to the celebrities they respect and will buy the products they use and endorse.*

So Mariani's recipe for success (fame+product=success) taught him a valuable lesson in celebrity endorsements that could

be repeated: people who "worshipped" the Pope ferociously bought the product the Pope recommended. He replicated the formula time and time again, and soon advertisements were appearing in publications all over the world, featuring hundreds of other celebrity endorsements, including some very famous figures of the day from all walks of life, such as the widely renowned French authors Jules Verne and Alexandre Dumas. One of his advertisements even offered to back up the claims, stating that the company would "mail gratis, 75 Portraits, Biographical Notes and Autographs of Celebrities, recommending 'Vin Mariani.'"

What, a bottle of tonic and a signed photograph of Dumas as well, who could ask for more?

Mariani's repeated his endorsement formula when the tonic hits the shores of the New World, where he sought out and engaged the leading scientist of the day, none other than Thomas Edison, to endorse the product. By this time, Edison was known across the globe as the creator of the carbon-powered lamp and as the person who harnessed electricity. Edison's influential endorsement proclaimed that Mariani's tonic helped him stay awake for long periods of time, ostensibly keeping him alert to make new discoveries and create new inventions.[4] With these efforts, Mariani created what was likely the first successful *multi-modal* celebrity endorsement campaign in America, unparalleled for its time, featuring multiple celebrities and using various media. He connected the strength of his product, *i.e.*, providing mental focus, with the strength of his endorser, *i.e.*, mental acuity. In this regard, he is also one of the first apparent marketers to create "singularity," a topic for later discussion. Mariani's campaign efforts helped the product achieve peak popularity throughout the States just as it had throughout the world.

Mariani's successful endorsement campaign would continue to reap significant rewards up until the advent of prohibition. Driven mostly by the Protestants in America, many

---

[4]Inciardi, James A. (1992). *The War on Drugs II.* Mayfield Publishing Company. p. 6

states passed laws in the early 1920's that outlawed the sale and production of alcoholic beverages in those jurisdictions, as well as its importation into the United States. This new era of restricting social behavior pitted the stricter Protestants, the "drys" as they were called, who opposed the evil influence of alcohol, against the so-called "wets" which included, among others, the Roman Catholics whose sacraments prominently featured the use of wine. Lest we forget, Pope Leo always had a flask of Vin Mariani in his hip pocket and had publically endorsed the "vile liquid" as it was described by the drys. With this historical development, the example of Mariani teaches us another great lesson regarding celebrity endorsements: *when the popularity and influence of your celebrity takes a nose dive, so often sales of the product they endorse also diminish.*

Prohibition affected the culture of America in many profound ways, but perhaps none less impactful than the creation of an entirely new product category. Rather than getting wrapped up in the debate or viewing it as a negative, this conflict of ethics between the Protestants and the Catholics was viewed as opportunity by John S. Pemberton, who enters the arena of history at this moment and forever changed America culture. Up to this time, Pemberton, a Southern gentleman, had produced an alcoholic product that competed closely with Mariani's tonic. But unlike Mariani, he anticipated the impending downward trend in an otherwise lucrative market and saw it as a way to monopolize that market. Rising above the conflicting social

14

morays surrounding the dispensable and controversial ingredient of alcohol, Pemberton took the initiative to develop a non-alcoholic, carbonated version of the beverage using those same coca leaves he and Mariani used in the alcoholic version. He called this new product *Coca-Cola*, and the rest, as they say, is history.

Like all great entrepreneurs, Pemberton studied his market and analyzed his competition routinely. So, to introduce the public to the new category of beverages, he took a page out of Mariani's book of success and used his marketing formulae, learning a valuable lesson from the downhill path that Mariani's endorsement from the Pope had taken. Pemberton understood the principle that the success or failure of a product often rises and falls with the success of its celebrity endorsers. Therefore, if your celebrity falls out of favor with the public, as did Pope Leo with his views on prohibition, so does your product, as did Mariani's tonic.

Pemberton realized that it wasn't the celebrity *endorsement* component of Mariani's formula that was flawed; it was the *celebrity* that became tainted. He asked himself, "What if a person could find a celebrity that would *never* become flawed or tainted?" So rather than hang the future of his new enterprise on a controversial celebrity such as Mariani's alcohol-imbibing Pope, Pemberton decided to create his very own celebrity endorser. Instead of using an actual person, who might be unpredictable, he designed an *illustration* of a celebrity whose image would be beyond reproach and, more importantly, one whose reputation and actions he could control implicitly. For that, he turned to an iconic legend that was more popular than the Pope, heck even more popular than Christ himself, the lovable St. Nicholas, or

"Santa Claus" for you moderns. This celebrity endorser still had the religious affectation of the Pope without any of the human flaws. So, in the 1920's, Pemberton began placing advertisements for Coca-Cola in the *Saturday Evening Post* featuring jolly images of Santa Clause guzzling down a bottle of his new concoction, along with memorable inscriptions like "My Hat's off to *the pause that refreshes.*"

Pemberton's addendums to Mariani's marketing formula – a fictional endorser and a memorable phrase – are features that are still being successfully used in marketing campaigns ranging from the Jolly Green Giant to the Geico lizard. Pemberton's endorsement from the fictional legend worked like Christmas magic, and the company ran these "Santa" campaigns for several decades. In fact, the Coca-Cola company still uses extensive holiday imagery as a major component of its marketing efforts and currently is parlaying the success of their Coca-Cola Polar Bears into a major Hollywood movie. Such efforts had a tremendous and deep impact on our culture, so much so that Coca-Cola's advertising imagery in those early years is often credited with the creation of our modern image of Santa Clause with his white beard and red suit, an image that is still prevalent around Christmas time in the malls and department stores.

So it is that celebrity endorsements have evolved from 3000 B.C., when the Roman gladiators helped sell gallons of olive oil to their adoring fans in the corridors of the Coliseum, to the 20th Century Santa Clause, who is portrayed in print advertisements pausing to enjoy a refreshing swig of his favorite cola. Of course, the evolution doesn't end there. The Coca-Cola campaigns, among many others, helped New York's Madison Avenue district grow from its humble beginning to its current status as the mecca of advertising and marketing, thus creating unique niches in the licensing of celebrity branding, persona, and trademarks. This led to the development of systems and methodologies for measuring the popularity of a celebrity in society as well as their potential effectiveness in a marketing campaign. Models have been created for determining whether a celebrity's perceived values line up with the values of a particular brand or product. Billions of dollars are poured into countless marketing campaigns like those launched during the Super Bowl, which brings us full circle in this historical cavalcade.

The Psychology of Celebrity Endorsement

Most everybody secretly imagines themselves in show business
and every day on their way to work,
they're a little bit depressed because they're not…
People are sad they're not famous in America.

-John Waters, *film producer*

John Waters' assessment that "everybody secretly imagines themselves" a celebrity and are "sad they're not famous" may, at first, seem overreaching or perhaps self-serving, but on careful examination it strikes at the heart and soul of America's fascination with celebrity, that being the psychological and genetic reasons for society's fascination with celebrity.

Abraham Lincoln once said "Character is like a tree and reputation like a shadow. The shadow is what we think of it; the tree is the real thing." If we juxtapose Lincoln's homespun quote with Waters' insight, we achieve a more complete illustration of the dichotomy between the public's perception of a celebrity, which according to Waters is who we wish to be, and the reality of what kind of person the celebrity actually is, *i.e.*, Lincoln's tree. This amalgam of their thoughts gives us an interesting glimpse into the psychological impact of celebrity endorsements.

In today's world of instant access, all types of information are broken into packets and disseminated with the push of button, flits about the digital network of pipelines, web pages, blogospheres and social media outlets, and is then consumed instantly by the masses of users when the bits coalesce on the other end on our computers and smartphones. Humankind has achieved *instant* gratification. For a price, anything can be obtained; if not instantly, within no more than two days with Amazon Prime (or perhaps within hours if Amazon establishes its proposed drone delivery network). Once 3-D printers become affordable and mainstream, a person will be able to "print" their products instantly at home!

This seemingly insatiable and unstoppable consumer drive and consumption fuels the ignoble need of most celebrities to be at the center of society's attention, so much so that they are willing to forego all privacy to seek out that attention. This form of symbiosis creates a veritable co-dependent state, but more on that later.

Psychologists who have studied how this willing loss of privacy that accompanies fame affects the celebrity over time confirm that celebrity's generally have a strong need for attention. One study explains that a celebrity experiences "fame" as a progression through four distinct phases, which are:

> "a period of *love/hate* towards the experience; an *addiction* phase where behavior is directly solely towards the goal of remaining famous; an *acceptance* phase, requiring a permanent change in everyday life routines; and finally an *adaptation* phase, where new

behaviors are developed in response to life changes involved in being famous."[5] (Emphasis added).

The more a celebrity enters the latter phases of this progression, the "adaptation" phase, the more that fame takes control and the celebrity can develop the idea that they are better or bigger than the "average" person, *i.e.* the non-celebrity. This attitude results in a desire to seek validation of their greatness from the fans, so a celebrity will eagerly establish direct connections with their fans through social media outlets such as Twitter, Facebook, and Instagram in an effort to connect with the approximately two billion points of potential consumption for their marketing and branding, that being the people on the Internet eager to digest the petabytes of available information about their favorite celebrities. These types of "intimate" connections creates a symbiotic relationship between the celebrity's desire for contemporaneous and instant disclosure, and the consumer's need for instant consumption, a cycle which can sometimes breed an environment for fanaticism in the fans and "symbolic immortality" in the celebrities, who believe it is their role to make an impact in the world. It is a cycle that propels itself internally through distinct co-dependent patterns. The result of this co-dependency created by social networking is that societal worship of celebrity has achieved a height that has never been achieved in the past.

---

[5] Rockwell, Donna and Giles, David C., "Being a Celebrity: A Phenomenology of Fame," *Journal of Phenomenological Psychology* 40 (2009) 178-210.

This symbiotic relationship creates the false perception in the mind of the fan that they know more about the celebrity than any other fan and that they have a unique relationship with the celebrity. Elvis Presley once said "the image is one thing and the human being is another. It's hard to live up to an image." Elvis' words poignantly recall Lincoln's homily, quoted earlier, which becomes particularly relevant: what the fan is actually observing is most often not the "real" celebrity, *i.e.*, their character/tree, but rather the "shadow" of their real self that is being projected by the celebrity or, more often than not, the celebrity's team of "handlers." To that point, frequently the social media posts are not even placed online by the celebrities themselves, but by interns or other hired Millenniums. That

 blind codependency is a powerful commodity in the hands of a skilled marketer.

The actual psychology underlying this symbiosis between celebrities and consumers is quite simple, even intuitive. It is based on the basic principle of classical, conditioned reflex response. Most people remember Ivan Pavlov's famous experiments in the early 1900's with what he called "psychic secretion." For those who never took remedial psychology, in his experimental trials, Pavlov would ring a bell each time he fed the test group of dogs, and

22

observe their immediate behavior to the external stimuli. He observed that after a period of time, the dogs would salivate at the tone of the bell, even if no food was introduced. The dogs had psychologically connected the external stimuli, the ring of the bell, with the internal satisfaction of being fed, so much so that even when the feeding was omitted, they still associated the *stimuli* with the *associated activity*. This basic psychological principle is diagramed in the following illustration:

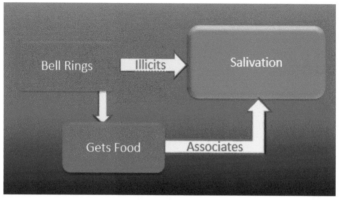

Illustration A

Society's fascination with celebrity is exploited by the industry to create a very similar stimulus. In scientific terms, the *British Journal of Psychology*, reported that psychologists had established a "sliding scale" of *celebrity fascination and fan behavior* on which the devoted fan becomes increasingly hooked onto the object of their attention until their feelings begin to resemble addiction. In other words, the stimuli of the celebrity's "shadow" is increasingly associated with the celebrity. Some experts in the field of fan behavior identify various increasing stages of such association as follows: admiring fan, fanatic, celebrity worship syndrome ("CWS") and erotomaniac.

The first level, an admiring fan, is a person who joins fan clubs and loyally buys products, while the next level, the fanatic, is the one who is a little more obsessed, perhaps clipping multiple articles about the celebrity and attending every concert or movie several times. These behaviors are fairly common and benign in psychological terms and are not considered socially unacceptable. However, fans who suffer from the greater levels of fascination - those with CWS or erotomaniacal behavior - present more elevated and sometimes dangerous fascinations with the celebrity. It may start out as CWS, with the fan perhaps believing that they are the celebrity's "soul mate," but this behavior often grows into the delusional idea in which the fan actually believes that he or she is romantically involved with the celebrity. The latter behavior is that of an erotomaniac, who often suffers from unnatural levels of the neurochemical serotonin.

The chemical process in the brain of those at these higher levels of fan fascination, CWS or Erotomaniacism, is very similar to that created when a drug addict craves a fix. They start out craving as much information about the celebrity as they can obtain. They are unceasing compelled by their imbalance to learn more, read more, and know more about the object of their favor. These levels of fascination are exacerbated by the details shared by celebrities through various forms of electronic interaction, particularly the various social media outlets discussed earlier.

Most popular celebrities routinely have fan bases of tens of millions of followers on these networks, breeding what is sometimes described casually as a "cult" following. For example, loyal female fans of the actor, Benedict Cumberbatch, known for his portrayal of Sherlock Holmes, are known as his "Cumberbitchs."

These celebrity cults are so prevalent that the *New Scientific* magazine reported that one third of all Americans suffer from some form of CWS. That means that one in every three American's suffer from some form of CWS. What is so startling about that statistic is that this extreme form of fanaticism that is present in 33% of our population often leads to the fans excessively craving the object of their attention, *i.e.*, the celebrity, and an even smaller subset of those fans afflicted with CWS will sometimes exhibit the erotomaniacal behavior that is anti-social or even dangerous.

Unfortunately, this psychological cult phenomenon may be embedded in our very DNA. One researcher, Stuart Fischoff, PhD, spokesman for the American Psychological Association and professor emeritus of media psychology at the California State University at Los Angeles, studied what he calls the "cult of celebrity." Dr. Fischoff believes that the "hero worship" exhibited by society is an evolved form of following the more important individual in our "pack," *i.e.*, the alpha male or female, which is sociologically coded into our genes. He points out that this programming feeds the celebrity centric focus in America, particularly in Hollywood, where the stars often get swept up in the mystique and encourage their "followers."[6] Fischoff describes the dependent cycle as cult behavior, and gives it the moniker the "celebrity cult."

When Pavlov's conditioned response is mixed with Dr. Fischoff's celebrity cult behavior, it creates a potent combination for exploiting the celebrity's persona through celebrity endorsements targeted at the fans. Make no mistake, marketers are very aware of these tendencies in American society and milk them for all they are worth. The result is that if a favorite celebrity is associated with a specific product through strategic use of the right media, the targeted fan will begin to associate the positive feelings they have for the celebrity with the endorsed product, in other words, they will have a reflexive response to the stimuli, hopefully at the point of sale, of course. The goal is to create a type of "singularity" between the product's image and the celebrity's image so that they are inextricable in the mind of the fan. This pattern, seen in Illustration B, reflects the same process Pavlov discovered:

---

[6] Carr, Coeli. *New Age of Celebrity Worship, Experts help you understand the good, the bad, and the ugly of being the world's biggest fan.* WebMD.com (Accessed March 2014).

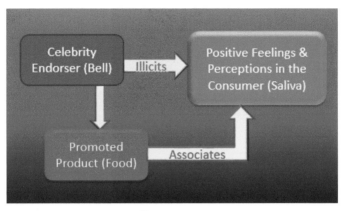

When a fan sees their favorite celebrity associated with a specific product (*i.e.,* when the bell is rung), the positive feeling and/or perceptions they have for the celebrity will be associated with the product (*i.e.,* they salivate), thus responding to something referred to in branding research as "singularity." Since the fan likely perceives that there is no other person in the world who is quite like the celebrity, they will perceive that the associated product, like the celebrity, is not quite like any other, but rather is exceptional. The respect they have for the celebrity is transferred seamlessly onto the product, and they essentially become one and the same. Understanding these psychological propensities, the marketer can use the fan's perception of the celebrity's image and values to help define, refresh, and add new dimensions to the brand's image and values, thereby building instant credibility for the brand as well as instant awareness and recall of the product. Who can think of the famous boxer George Foreman now without recalling the George Foreman Grill? In fact, recent market research finding indicate that eight out of ten television commercials scoring the highest in consumer recall featured celebrity appearances.

The Apple corporation uses these principals in their highly effective marketing strategies. It begins with a well-designed logo, something discussed at great length in a  subsequent chapter. In this case, the successful efforts of the computer giant are compressed into their trademark Apple with a bite taken out of the side. The Apple is usually either silhouetted or glowing, as it does on the cover of every laptop they have produced since the first MacBook Pro. What does this shining image portray to the consumer? First, it conveys simplicity: Apple's computers are as easy to understand and use as, well an apple. It is literally the modern day equivalent of Eve's temptation to Adam and a direct implementation of Pavlovian stimuli. Go ahead, take a bite, you know you want it. Second, the simplicity of the logo subtlety conveys a very Zen-like, natural but well-thought-out design, a corporate emphasis the company has worked hard to convey. What feels better in your hand than a smooth, sweet apple?

Next, Apple incorporates that imagery and stimuli into their advertisement by carefully choosing the celebrities used for their endorsements.   Some of their successful campaigns included, for example, Bob Dylan and Martin Scorsese, each individual unique in their respective mediums of music and film. Dylan is the iconic poet and songwriter and Scorsese the iconic filmmaker. Both celebrities fit squarely in Apple's wheelhouse, highlighting various facets of the corporate philosophy and

imagery portrayed in their trademark. The fans of each of these celebrities are also particularly interesting in certain segments of the marketplace in which Apple has traditionally excelled, music and graphics. So, each celebrity

weaves in elements of marketing strategy that subtlety positions the brand as distinctive and unique.   Apple enhances the connection by employing the same silhouetting techniques used in the creation of their logo. As the illustration of Bob Dylan shows, he is silhouetted on a simple Zen-like blue screen in order to draw the comparison to Apple more vividly.

While it may be difficult to argue with Apple's success in marketing, their methodologies are not new, as the examples of Mariani, Pemberton and Pavlov illustrates. If nothing else, our foray into the annals of history showed us that the effects of good celebrity endorsement efforts are imminently repeatable and based on sound psychological principles. The strong psychological attachment that develops between a brand and a celebrity sometimes forms such an inextricable association that it is difficult to think of one without thinking of the other. In some instances, the product line or brand can integrate with the persona of the celebrity so much so that the brand actually becomes a celebrity in its own right. Thus, the brand and the celebrity achieve singularity, defined earlier, *i.e.*, the perceptual linkage between the values of the celebrity and the brand. To illustrate this, think of the names Michael Jordan, Ed McMann, Bill Cosby, John Madden and the aforementioned George Foreman. If you are like the majority of consumers, your mind almost instantly went to Air Jordan, Publisher's House Sweepstakes, Jell-O, EA Sports' Madden Football, and the George Foreman Grill respectively, even before you recalled the successful careers each had respectively in basketball, announcing, acting, coaching, and boxing. Those celebrities are forever bound to the products with which they became associated. They are one. That is singularity.

As apparent as the psychological and sociological effects of celebrity endorsements appear, they were nonetheless empirically confirmed by Friedman & Friedman in 1979, whose research specifically concluded that the use of celebrity endorsements psychologically leads to greater believability and more positive purchase intention.[7] In short, the end goal of every celebrity endorsement campaign is to increase exposure to a brand and/or sell some product or service to the consumer by creating an affiliation with the celebrity's fan base, thereby creating singularity. Those consumers come in all shapes and sizes, all beliefs, and all cultures, as do the celebrities those consumers adore. So, if the brand can align with a celebrity whose values and lifestyle match that of the product, they know that the consumers who are fans of that celebrity (the "ringing bell") will most likely buy the product they are trying to sell (the "food"). Not only can they be conditioned to draw the association, but even more compelling, it is programmed into their DNA to "follow the leader." In a subsequent chapter, we will examine specific methodologies for determining which particular celebrity a company should employ with regard to various products, but for now suffice it say that these background psychological principles help determine the proper celebrity to use for a particular campaign. The key is to find a celebrity whose values are perceived by your target market to align closely to their own values.

---

[7] Friedman, H.H. & Friedman, L., Endorser Effectiveness by Product Type, *Journal of Advertising Research*, 19(3) 1979, pp. 63-71.

Celebrity Persona & Rights of Publicity

I have always been famous;, it's just [that] no one knew me yet.
-Lady Gaga

The psychology underlying celebrity endorsements is interesting from an academic and historical standpoint, but it raises the legal question of "what gives the celebrity a legal right to exploit his or her fame?" The rights of a celebrity to license their persona – their name, likeness, image, signature and other attributes - is based on the legal concept of a person's "rights of publicity." The right of publicity is the personal right of *any individual* to control the commercial use of his or her name, likeness, or other unequivocal aspects of their identity. So Lady Gaga was correct that she has "always been famous" in the sense that she has always had that right to her persona, just as you do.

But, if you read the amendments to the United States Constitution, our Bill of Rights, you will not find the "right of publicity" listed among the rights enumerated there, as you do for our First Amendment right to free speech, religion and peaceable assembly, our Second Amendment right to bear arms, or our Fourth Amendment protections against illegal search and seizure. Instead, the right of publicity has developed in the common law court system and, over time, in various state statutes. In this chapter, we will examine the evolution of the legal right of publicity and explore its derivation.

Many attribute the phrase "right of publicity" to Judge Jerome Frank, who is said to have introduced the phrase into American vernacular in *Haelean Laboratories, Inc. v. Topps Chewing Gum, Inc.*[8] In this decision, Judge Frank correctly observed the converse relationship between the "right of publicity" and the "right of privacy." New York's publicity law, which was being applied by Judge Frank to the case, enabled individuals to protect themselves from unauthorized commercial appropriation of their personal attributes. In the *Topps Chewing Gum* case, Judge Frank recognized in the privacy right a broader, independent right protecting the economic interests of a person, rather than the personal, emotional interests traditionally associated with the right of privacy.

Judge Frank clearly articulated the relationship between these two rights. So, as counterintuitive as it might sound upon initial impression, the right of publicity in the United States is the "flip side" of a legal coin called the "right of privacy": the two are logically and inextricably related, yet clearly distinct. Simply put, if people have the right to protect the attributes associated with their persona from being exposed to the public (the right of privacy), then logically they have the converse right to exploit those attributes as well (the right of publicity). These two categories of rights are sometimes grouped together in the broader phrase "personality rights." So inasmuch as we have a

---

[8] 202 F.2d 866 (2nd Cir. 1953).

Constitutional right of privacy, it stands to reason that the right of publicity is a Constitutional right, even if our Forefathers did not specifically identify it as such in the Bill of Rights.

Opponents of intellectual property rights as well as those inclined to a stricter interpretation of the Constitution would disagree with my conclusion here that there is a right of privacy supported in the Bill of Rights, pointing to the fact that, at least on the surface, the amendments are peculiarly silent when it comes to such a right. But if the Bill of Rights is analyzed closely and consideration is given to the original intent, the privacy right can be seen glistening through, like a ray of sun streaming through the keyhole of a darkened door.

In a *Harvard Law Review* article written in 1890, Samuel D. Warren and Louis D. Brandeis, both law students at the time, aggressively defended the fact that a person has the Constitutional right "to be left alone." The article has since become one of the seminal treatises on the privacy right. Later, as a Supreme Court justice Brandeis defended the right in a dissenting opinion in the wire-tapping case of *Olmstead v. United States* (1928),[9] where the majority opinion by Chief Justice Howard Taft erroneously ruled that wiretapping private telephone conversations, with subpoenas obtained by federal agents without judicial approval, did not violate the 4th

---

[9] 277 U.S. 438 (1928).

Amendment's prohibition against illegal search and seizure.[10] In that dissent, Justice Brandeis posed the question: "Can it be that the Constitution affords no protection against such invasions of individual security?" His answer to that question expanded those early ideas formulated in his law school treatise into what is now understood to be our Constitutional right of privacy. There is currently little doubt as the existence of such a right, even for those who cling to a literal interpretation of the Constitution. Specifically, Brandeis wrote, in the most often quoted section of the *Olmstead* opinion, that

> "The makers of our Constitution understood the need to secure conditions favorable to the pursuit of happiness, and the protections guaranteed by this are much broader in scope, and include the right to life and an inviolate personality -- *the right to be left alone* -- the most comprehensive of rights and the right most valued by civilized men . . ."

While it was Justice Brandeis who first recognized the existence of a right of privacy in the Bill of Rights, the right has been supported by every Supreme Court as a component of Constitutional rights ever since the *Katz* opinion overturned *Olmstead* and proclaimed that every U.S. citizen is entitled to a "reasonable expectation of privacy." As Brandeis stated, "the principals underlying the Fourth and Fifth Amendments is protection against invasions of the sanctities of a man's home and

---

[10] The *Olmstead* decision was later overturned by the Supreme Court in *Katz v. United States*, 389 U.S. 347 (1967), which extended Fourth Amendment protection to all areas where a person has a "reasonable expectation of privacy."

privacies of life." Here Brandeis recognizes that the Bill of Rights implicitly reflects the desires of its architect, James Madison, to protect certain components of basic human existence, privacy foremost among them. Brandeis concludes that "[t]his is a recognition of the significance of man's spiritual nature, his feelings, and his intellect." From that perspective, the rights of privacy and publicity might be thought of as an "intellectual property" right, very much akin to the guarantee of a monopoly in "intellectual property" found in the Progress Clause: Article 1, Section 8, Clause 8 of our Constitution. It could be argued, then, that even more so than a person's intellect and feelings, a person's name, likeness and other indicia of their person are significant.

This analysis reveals that privacy rights can be found throughout the Bill of Rights, revealing the thoughts of Madison as he crafted them. For example, the First Amendment's protection of the freedom of speech and to exercise religion protects one's ability to keep personal beliefs private as well as one's ability to publicly express them. Further, the Third and Fourth Amendments protect the privacy and sanctity of one's home from being illegally searched, seized and/or used to quarter soldiers. In addition, the Fourth Amendment also serves to protect the privacy of our "persons . . . papers and effects." Our right of privacy is also implicitly protected by the Ninth Amendment, which states specifically that the "enumeration in the Constitution, of certain rights, shall not be construed to deny or disparage others retained by the people." Finally, and perhaps most importantly, the Fourteenth Amendment guarantees that no United States citizen shall be deprived of "life, liberty or property" without due process, a clause which has been used by the Supreme Court to guarantee a right of privacy in cases ranging from procreation to termination of medical treatment.

There are two earlier decisions originating from the same Taft court which decided the *Olmstead* case that also inform our study on rights of privacy. These two cases interpreted the liberty clause to prohibit states from interfering with the private decisions of educators and parents to shape the education of children: *Meyer v Nebraska* (1923)[11] and *Pierce v. Society of Sisters* (1925).[12] Writing for the 7-member majority in *Meyer*, Justice McReynolds explained the application of the Fourteenth Amendment:

> "While this court has not attempted to define with exactness the liberty thus guaranteed, the term has received much consideration and some of the included things have been definitely stated. . . . Without doubt, it denotes not merely freedom from bodily restraint but also the right of the individual to contract, to engage in any of the common occupations of life, to acquire useful knowledge, to marry, establish a home and bring up children, to worship God according to the dictates of his own conscience, and generally to enjoy those privileges long recognized at common law as essential to the orderly pursuit of happiness by free men."[13]

---

[11] 262 U.S. 390 (1923).
[12] 268 U.S. 510 (1925).
[13] 262 U.S. at 399.

These early Supreme Court cases regarding a privacy right gained a new head of steam during the Warren Court of the Sixties, which focused heavily on personal rights. In 1965, the Court decided the seminal case of *Griswold v Connecticut*[14] on the basis of an established right of privacy, striking down a state law prohibiting the possession, sale, and distribution of contraceptives to married couples. Justice William O. Douglas saw various "penumbras" and "emanations" of the right of privacy in the Bill of Rights and concluded that the amendments create, in his words, "a zone of privacy," a catch phrase that is still frequently featured in Supreme Court jurisprudence. Those emanations and penumbras reflect the philosophy of Madison. Decades later, the Supreme Court has emphatically and definitively connected the Fourteenth Amendment's guarantee of *liberty and the pursuit of happiness* to a right of privacy. In the 2003 case of *Lawrence v. Texas,*[15] Justice Kennedy concludes that "choices central to personal dignity and autonomy, are central to the liberty protected by the Fourteenth Amendment. Thus, the Supreme Court has firmly established this "zone of privacy" as a realm of personal liberty into which the government cannot enter and our privacy rights hinge on this reasonable expectation of privacy.[16]

---

[14] 381 U.S. 479 (1965).
[15] 539 U.S. 558 (2003).
[16] William L. Prosser, Privacy, 48 Cal. L. Rev. 383, 383 (1960).

This line of legal decisions clearly illustrates an acknowledgement by the Supreme Court that the concept of privacy was an implicit thread that ran throughout Madison's expressions as he drafted the Constitutional Amendments. It was almost as if Madison believed that privacy is *such an obvious right* that it didn't need a direct reference to the guarantee. Nonetheless, the right of privacy echoes throughout the entire Bill of Rights like a voice calling out in the darkness, not immediately apparent but extremely present. And once we discover the right of privacy, its logical twin sibling, "the right of publicity," cannot be far behind.

So the rights of privacy, and by inference the right of publicity, are featured in the American cultural *zeitgeist* by this pantheon of great thinkers, from the philosophy of Locke as infused in the writings of Madison, Jefferson, and other Founding Fathers, right on down through to its direct application by Justices Warren, Brandeis, and others. These two rights are, in fact, rooted in philosophies that are more ancient than these great thinkers of the Supreme Court. They are very much grounded in the philosophy of the 18th-century thinker Immanuel Kant and others like him, and even before Kant in the Greek philosophies passed down in Aristotle's Academy, and in the teaching and writings of Cicero. Thomas Jefferson paid homage to all of these predecessors when he recognized that the inspiration for our founding documents is based on "harmonizing sentiments of the day, whether expressed in conversation, in letters, printed essays, or the elementary books of public right, as Aristotle, Cicero, Locke, Sidney, etc.," which he described as *"an expression of the American mind."* So our Founding Fathers, as well as the Supreme Court justices who interpret them, are building on a foundation of thought about personhood and privacy that was generated by the earliest of thinkers and flows throughout the thought of many generations of thinkers, right on through to the present day.

From these great thinkers our Founding Fathers learned that an individual has an inherent right to choose for his or her self. Indeed, according to these philosophers, what distinguished human beings from mere animals who act solely on the basis of instinct and, ironically stimuli, is that human beings possess the ability to freely choose what they will do with their lives. More importantly, they possess an inherent dignity and a fundamental moral right to have these choices respected. These concepts of human dignity and integrity play a significant role throughout history, particularly in Enlightenment thought, in our right of privacy, as do notions of individual autonomy and self-determination. Consequently, people are not objects to be manipulated by other people, and it is a basic violation of human dignity to use people in ways they do not freely choose. In this sense, it is very much a personal right. In fact, this philosophy of natural rights is the basis of all our *personal rights* in the U.S., but as specifically applied to our right of privacy, we have the right to do, believe, and say whatever we choose to do, believe, or say in our personal lives so long as we do not violate those same basic rights of others.

The enlightenment philosopher John Locke, a proponent of natural rights, also believed that each individual has the right to control his or her "own body" as did the Greek philosophers, but he extended the right to include the "fruits" produced by that body. We can extend that line of thinking even further to postulate that the same "body" has the right to control how his or her persona is used, whether it be controlled for private relationship only or exploited publicly for commercial gain. This applies directly to a celebrity's rights to exploit their persona. Substantial amounts of time, money, and effort are expended to develop a celebrity's prominence in a particular segment of the entertainment industry, whether it be music, television, movies, sports, or whatever. Take Roger Federer as an example: Roger is widely recognized as the best in his business, perhaps the greatest tennis player that ever lived. He achieved this fame not only with his God-given talent, but also with hard work, practice, family support, and the expenditure of much energy and investment. Certainly, the licensing and endorsement deals which generate a substantial percentage of his livelihood are the well-deserved fruits of his labor. So in this sense, the rights of publicity more closely resemble a *real property* right, *e.g.*, the right to own land or a home, than it does the personal rights of Aristotle and Cicero, as enumerated in the Bill of Rights. But more on this in the next chapter. Either way, it is clear that our rights of publicity are inextricably intertwined with our rights of privacy.

As clear as it is, this intertwined relationship between rights of privacy and publicity creates confusion, as is evident in the application of the principles by state legislators across the United States. Because there is no clearly applicable Federal law, all legislation concerning rights of publicity falls squarely in state-based law and therefore its recognition varies from state to state, sometimes in large measure. While most states recognize the more-established right of privacy, not all recognize the closely-related, but less common, right of publicity.

To date, little more than half of the fifty United States recognize some form of the right of publicity, either in their common laws or by a direct statute: seventeen states specifically recognize some form of the right of publicity in a specific statute,[17] while at least eleven others have recognized the right in their common law court decisions.[18]

New York courts led the way in the development of rights of publicity law in the United States in a case dating all the way back to 1902,[19] involving Abigail Roberson, a minor. Without her

---

[17] California, Florida, Hawaii, Illinois, Indiana, Kentucky, Massachusetts, Nebraska, Nevada, New York, Oklahoma, Rhode Island, Tennessee, Utah, Virginia, Washington and Wisconsin.

[18] Alabama, Arizona, Connecticut, Georgia, Michigan, Minnesota, Missouri, New Jersey, Ohio, Pennsylvania and Texas.

[19] *Roberson v. Rochester Folding Box Co.*, 171 N.Y. 538, 64 N.E. 442 (N.Y. 1902).

knowledge or consent, the Franklin Mills Co. began using Ms. Roberson's image on bags of flour, marketing materials, lithographic prints and photos, which they publically displayed in stores and salons that sold the product. All totaled, the defendant distributed over 25,000 copies of Abigail's image, all manufactured by the Rochester Folding Box Co. Ms. Roberson's complaint against Franklin Mills and Rochester Box Co., based on the then-novel concept of rights of privacy, sought $15,000 in damages as well as an injunction prohibiting further distribution. She was ultimately awarded damages for her pain and suffering.[20]

This *Rochester Folding Box* case led to the enactment of the New York Civil Right Law by the state legislature in 1903, §§ 50 and 51 of which prohibit the use of the name, portrait, or picture of any living person without prior consent for "advertising purposes" or "for the purposes of trade." Violation of this statute is a criminal misdemeanor, but Section 51 also gives a person a right to pursue civil action if their persona is exploited without their permission. There are several important lessons to take from this case and the resulting legislation: (1) that rights of publicity can be protected through both the exercise of common law principles, as in the litigation, and statute, and (2) that the rights of publicity are not the exclusive domain of the celebrity, but rather can be applied by citizens who are not famous.

---

[20] Spears, Victoria Prussen, *The Case That Started it All: Roberson v. Rochester Folding Box Co.*, Privacy & Data Security Law Journal, November 2008.

Some states, such as Tennessee, California, Kentucky, Utah and Wisconsin for example, do, in fact, recognize *both* a statutory and common law right of publicity. So if we broaden our analysis to include actions based on all forms of torts, a total of more than forty states recognize some form of right of publicity tort actions based on common law, statute, or both.[21]

The elements of the common law tort for violation a person's right of publicity vary from state to state, but in general, the most common components include: (1) the use of a person's name, identity or persona (some state include signature, photographs, voice, and other identifying characteristics as well); (2) the use of that right of publicity by the defendant for commercial gain (through advertisement and/or commercial activity) and; (3) without the consent or license of the person; that (4) causes some sort of injury to the plaintiff. These common law principles can be applied in Federal courts too, as in the case involving a Samsung advertisement entitled "The Longest Running Game Show 2012" that humorously featured the *Wheel of Fortune* tile turner, Vanna White, as a futuristic robot wearing a blonde wig. The 9th Circuit found that California's common law rights of publicity not only protect Ms. White's identity, but "anything that evokes [the celebrity's] personality" as well.[22]

---

[21] Sager, Kellie L., and Tremaine, David Wright. *Summary of Rights of Publicity Issues.*
[22] *Vanna White v. Samsung Electronics America, et al.*, 971 F.2d 1395 (9th Cir. 1992). In a similar action decided almost a decade earlier, the Sixth

All of this variation among the states leads to the conclusion that there is a definitive need for Federal guidance relating to personality rights, perhaps a law similar to other intellectual property statutes such as the Copyright Act of 1976, the Trademark Act of 1952 (the "Lanham Act"), or the Patent Act of 1946, but there is a veritable drought when we look to the Federal government for assistance.

As for the highest court in our land, there is only one specific reference to a right of publicity in the annals of the Supreme Court of the United States. In 1977, the Supremes decided the seminal case of *Zacchini v. Scripps-Howard Broadcasting.* Zacchini involved "The Great Hugo," a famous human cannonball who sued Scripps-Howard for displaying his entire 15-second live performance on the local television news program. He argued that the intrinsic value of his act depended on the public's desire to witness the event, so displaying the entire event on television essentially eliminated the desire of the public to come out in person and pay to see it. In language reminiscent of the policies that support other intellectual property laws, Justice White supported Zacchini's "right of publicity" using language that could easily be the mission statement for copyright law, defending it in order to provide "an economic incentive for him to

---

Circuit ruled that Johnny Carson's claim against a portable toilet manufacturer who advertised using his signature phrase "Here's Johnny" was liable for violating his rights of publicity. *Carson v. Here's Johnny Portable Toilets, Inc.,* 698 F.2d. 831 (6th Cir. 1983).

make the investment required to produce a performance of interest to the public."[23]

The *Zacchini* decision planted the right of publicity squarely in the realm of intellectual property law where it belongs. In particular, there are some noteworthy similarities between the right of publicity and trademark law. Specifically, the right of publicity is of the same genus as unfair competition and, more precisely, the doctrine of misappropriation and/or false designation of origin, hallmarks of trademark law reflected in the Lanham Act.[24]

Similar to the function of a company's trademark, a celebrity's right of publicity functions as assurance to a consumer of the quality of the celebrity's performance, *i.e.*, they know what to expect. A right of publicity also allows the celebrity to prevent others from reaping unjust rewards by appropriation of the celebrity's ostensibly well-deserved fame. The Lanham Act makes a person liable in court if that person uses a celebrity's name in connection with goods or services if the person gives a false impression that the celerity is somehow associated.

This foundational trademark principle generally holds true even in those eleven jurisdictions where the right of publicity is relegated to common law, however, in those states a person may have to rely on more traditional tort principles such as "passing

---

[23] 433 U.S. 562, 576 (1977).
[24] 15 U.S. Code §1125

off" or "pawning off" a trade name, risk of consumer confusion, or some form of unfair competition.

While the use of these trademark principles to support a claim for rights of publicity is a powerful tool, the drawback is that it may limit the celebrity to the use of his or her name in association with goods and services. As a result, these techniques do not bestow the same level of protection offered by the broader rights of publicity statutes in those states that recognize them. In fact, courts that allow celebrity claims on the basis of the Lanham Act typically apply the same eight-factor analysis used in most trademark infringement actions, requiring some evidence of consumer confusion.[25] This is sometimes a very formidable task. In contrast, cases prosecuted under state rights of publicity statutes do not suffer from the same strict analysis as under the more stringent trademark analysis.

This close relationship between trademark and rights of publicity reflects the recent nomenclature of "branding" a personality, something we'll explore in detail later. Traditionally, the term "brand" was practically synonymous with a company's trademark. In today's media driven world, a celebrity's fame is

---

[25] The factors were developed (pun intended) in *Polaroid Corp. v. Polarad Elect. Corp.*, 287 F.2d 492 (2d Cir. 1961), and are: (1) the strength of his mark; (2) the degree of similarity between the two marks; (3) the proximity of the products and/or services; (4) the likelihood that the prior owner will bridge the gap; (5) actual confusion among consumers; (6) the defendant's good faith in adopting its own mark; (7) the quality of the defendant's product; and (8) the sophistication of the buyers.

crafted and honed to the point where many celebrities also equate their personas as a type of brand.

As Locke's philosophy teaches us with regard to copyright, a celebrity's fame is ultimately the result of that celebrity's hard work, talent, and investment, and they should profit from the fruits of their labor. This brings us back into the realm of intellectual property, where the words of the great father of copyright, Melville Nimmer, written in 1954, are a particularly appropriate place to summarize:

> [E]very person is entitled to the fruit of his labors unless there are important countervailing public policy considerations. Yet, because of the inadequacy of traditional legal theories . . . persons who have long and laboriously nurtured the fruit of publicity values may be deprived of them, unless judicial recognition is given to what is here referred to as the right of publicity—that is, the right of each person to control and profit from the publicity values which he has created or purchased.[26]

Rather than "judicial recognition," as Nimmer suggest here, what this patchwork quilt of state law, common law, torts and federal jurisprudence regarding personality rights actually illustrates more clearly is the dramatic need for consistent application that can only come in the form of a Federal law regarding rights of publicity. Until that time, the U.S. will continue to see inconsistent application of this basic right.

---

[26] Melville B. Nimmer, "The Right of Publicity," 19 *Law & Contemp. Probs.* 203, 216 (1954)

The Intersection of Free Speech with Personal Rights: Celebrity Impersonators

In 2011 the IRS reported that 84,000 people in the U.S. listed their occupation on their tax returns as "Elvis impersonator." Does a person have the right to "express" themselves by dressing up as a celebrity such as Elvis and impersonating them? Does it matter whether or not the impersonator earns money by performing as the celebrity? These questions cannot be answered without understanding how intellectual property intersects with the First Amendment. All intellectual property rights must be balanced against the First Amendment right of free speech. Copyright is limited by the balancing the defense of "fair use," whereas patent is limited by the "staple article" doctrine. Both of these legal doctrines are examples of how Lady Justice balances the two rights on her scales of justice. The right of publicity is no exception, and certainly has its own share of limitations and exceptions. There is an inherent tension between an individual's right to control the use of his or her identity and the free dissemination of speech and ideas guaranteed to society by our Forefathers in the First Amendment. In this chapter, well explore this tension created when free speech rights intersect with personal rights in the form of celebrity impersonations, which require us to balance the impersonator's free speech rights against the celebrity personal rights.

Old Navy ran a television advertisement in 2011 featuring a brunette with a heart-shaped face and her hair swept to one side in a ponytail. The commercial was campy, featuring the brunette happily carrying shopping bags and singing joyfully as she road in the back of a convertible. The model used in the advertisement, Melissa Molinaro, bore a striking resemblance to a more famous diva, Kim Kardashian – too striking for Kardashian. In a lawsuit involving the Old Navy advertisement, Kardashian claimed the

resemblance was no accident, but that the look-alike was used intently to conjure up images of her. She filed the complaint in  Federal court alleging, among other things, misappropriation of her rights of publicity and trademarks. Kardashian sought $20 million in damages.

According to the complaint, the advertisement featured Molinaro wearing Kardashian's trademark hairdo and a distinct imitation of Kardashian's campy personality. Old Navy defended the action on First Amendment grounds, claiming that any appropriation of Kardashian's persona or trademarks was a parody, protected by the principle of fair use. This case was somewhat complicated by the fact that Molinaro was dating one of Kardashian's ex-boyfriends which, while weird in a soap opera sort of way, is really irrelevant. The question a trier of fact would have had to decide is whether Kardashian's persona and reputation has commercial values and, if so, did the impersonation tarnish that reputation. Unfortunately, this case does not provide any legal insight, as it was settled out of court and the details are undisclosed, although the fact that the advertisement was removed from YouTube is some indication that it was likely settled in Kardashian's favor. It does, however, clearly illustrate the balance that must be maintained between

personal and free speech rights.

This issue of imitation and free speech rights can be exacerbated by the fact that Hollywood is fond of casting actors who resemble past celebrities. In fact, if you compare photos of Kim Kardashian to Glee actress Naya River, the resemblance is uncanny, so an equally persuasive argument perhaps could have been advanced that Molinaro was imitating River rather than Kardashian. I spent most my time watching 2015's Oscar-nominated movie *The Imitation Game* having to

remind myself that supporting actress Keira Knightley, pictured to left, was, in fact, *not* Wynonna Ryder, pictured to the right. In these situations, where an actress

resembles a popular, older actress, the First Amendment principle is obvious: Knightley has as much of a free speech right to practice her craft as does Wynonna in spite of the uncanny resemblance.

The more difficult questions arise when, as in the case of Molinaro, an attempt is made to "trick" the public into believing that they are looking at Kim Kardashian. Does Molinaro, an actress, have as much a right to practice her craft as does Kardashian by playing a role that makes the public believe that Kardashian is endorsing Old Navy. This intent to subtlety play off a celebrity's fame to persuade Kardashian's fans to purchase a product she doesn't endorse tips the scales of justice in favor of the intellectual property rights being infringed, and outweighs the limiting principles of free speech. In this instance, the free speech rights are offset by the rights of publicity.

This analysis of balancing two types of rights against each other is applied in more typical First Amendment cases. Do I have the free speech right, for example, to post a billboard on my own property that defames a neighbor and states a falsehood or is that outweighed by the personal rights of my neighbor to not be defamed? While the Bill of Rights clearly states that "Congress shall make no law . . ." restricting freedom of expression, subsequent interpretations have restricted expression in certain circumstances such as this one. When an expression is likely to cause harm to an individual and their relationships with others, the law will often choose to protect those individual's rights over the right of society to free speech. Specifically, the Supreme Court has ruled that rights of publicity should prevail over free speech when necessary to prevent someone who has "stolen" a celebrity's good will and derived something for free from the celebrity that has intrinsic value and for which, under normal circumstances, the thief would have to pay. In other words, if the use of the celebrity's persona is for commercial purposes, such as advertising some product or service, or the celebrity's name or likeness is used on merchandise, that type of commercial expression generally will not be protected by the First Amendment.

The intentional act of an impersonator dressing up like a celebrity creates one set of issues, but the more intriguing analysis involves the freedom of expression issues that arise from the so-called "doppelganger" cases like the Ryder/Knightley example above. The word doppelganger is an Anglicized form of the German doppelgänger, translated "double goer," referring to a person who is physically and/or behaviorally identical to another person. This concept was popularized as a running theme interspersed throughout the long-running CBS sitcom, *How I Met Your Mother*, during which each of the main characters in the show discovered their doppelgangers during various episodes.

You may anticipate where this going: legally, issues arise when the doppelganger of a celebrity chooses to exploit their similarity for financial gain. Like the impersonator, the doppelganger certainly has a Constitutional right to exist and earn a living, even if it is by imitating the celebrity. The problem clearly illustrates the concept of balancing this right against the right of the celebrity to his or her "brand" when the doppelganger's intent is to deceive the public.

In 2005 an agent for a Las Vegas doppelganger who looked like Robin Williams, the now deceased comedian/actor, set up an interview for the impersonator with a newspaper columnist and the organizer of a fire department charity event. The news columnist admits that she was "completely suckered" by the doppelganger's hairy harms, his mock Minnesota accent (a frequent routine of Williams), and his impersonation of Mrs. Doubtfire. Clayton's motives were  questionable, as he performs a show called *Rockin' Robin*, a "one-man comedy and musical comedy audience interaction show" in which he impersonates Williams. Upon learning of this, Williams sued Clayton in a Federal court in Minnesota accusing him of violating his rights of publicity, false advertising, and other related claims. Four months into the case, the parties settled the case without damages, with Clayton agreeing to a Court Order that bars him from imitating Williams "without expressly informing [his] actual and potential audiences, regardless of size or location, that [he] is not the real Robin Williams." The case again illustrates the established principle that a person has a free speech right to imitate a celebrity, but does not have the right to deceive the public into thinking that he or she is the celebrity.

56

This attempt to deceive the public is what has been referred to as "passing off," *i.e.*, a person does not have the right to pass themselves off as the celebrity. This common law tort, developed primarily in courts in the United Kingdom, is frequently used to enforce unregistered trademark rights and to protect the goodwill of the owner of the intellectual property by preventing someone else from misrepresenting the goods or services as being the goods and services of another or from holding out his or her goods or services as having an association or connection the owner.

Since the rights of persona fall into the realm of intellectual property, like trademark and copyright, the passing off principle is "borrowed," as it were, from the world of trademark and is a very important and powerful tool to enforce a celebrity's right of publicity. A doppelganger may exploit his or her own persona by performing as an impersonator so long as he or she makes appropriate disclaimers, or it is apparent that they are NOT the celebrity, and does not offer the impression to the public that the celebrity is endorsing either the performance, a product or service, or anything related to the doppelganger. This balancing of rights insures the protection of both the celebrity's right of publicity and the doppelganger's right to free expression and to earn a living.

Along these same lines, the question often arises as to whether someone whose voice sounds identical to a celebrity's voice may use it for commercial purposes, that is, can he or she work as a "voice over" artist. Since the voice is one of the most identifiable characteristics of a person's right of publicity, many of the state statutes regarding rights of publicity specifically identify the voice as one of a person's characteristics that can be protected. The deep voice of a prominent celebrity such as James Earl Jones or Ving Rhames can fetch millions of dollars, whereas the similar voice of an imitator will only cost thousands. For this reason, advertising agencies often skate on thin ice when they utilize vocal imitators to reproduce the distinctive voice of the celebrity in order to side step paying that particular celebrity the market value his or her voice would normally command.

Whereas it is more difficult to enforce the right of a celebrity to prevent a "sound alike" from working as a voice over artist, the more definitive examples arise in the instance of celebrity singers. In 1988, Ford created an original advertising campaign featuring famous songs from the 1970's, usually sung by their original artists. However, if the original artists refused to license the use of the original sound recording or to participate in the campaign, Ford hired impersonators whose voices sounded like the original recording artists to record the original songs for use in the commercials. Most of these artists were on the long tail of their career and welcomed the opportunity, but when Ford approached Bette Midler she refused. So Ford hired a voice-over artist who sounded like Midler and used the song for the commercial without her permission. It is important to note that Ford did, in fact, obtain permission from the owner of the copyright in the *musical composition*, so the issue is centered squarely on Midler's rights of publicity. In that regard, it is also important to point out that Midler's image and likeness were not used in the commercial, so the case was focused solely on her voice and sound.

Ford did an excellent job with the imitation: most people who saw the advertisement agreed that the voice-over artist sounded identical to Midler. Midler was not happy, so she sued Ford in a California district court for misappropriation of her voice and sought damages for the use of her intellectual property. The District Court denied her claim, however, so she promptly appealed to the 9th Circuit Court of Appeals. The 9th Circuit reversed the District Court's decision. The appeal court's opinion reinforced what we have seen throughout the chapter: Ford's act of intentionally impersonating Midler's voice without her permission was the equivalent of taking her identity, and when such a recognized voice is deliberately replicated for commercial use, the imitators are liable for violating her rights of publicity.

A similar fact pattern occurred a few years later when a singer imitating Tom Waits used one of his trademark songs in a Doritos commercial. Waits has a very distinctive "sandpaper" baritone quality in his voice that brings out subtle nuances on ballads, which has generated much acclaim as well as a huge cult following. Frito Lay's use of a Waits sound alike to perform one of his songs was a deliberate and intentional attempt to draw support for its product from Waits' fan base. In that case, no surprise, the 9th Circuit upheld a $2.5-million-dollar jury verdict for Waits based on the same principles it declared in the Midler decision.

Waits is notoriously aggressive about protecting his distinctive voice, and for obvious commercial reasons. It is, after all, literally his bread and butter. In 2006, Waits was awarded damages in a situation to the Frito-Lay case, in which Audi used his song *Innocent When You Dream* using a sound alike. Waits currently has several other similar cases pending around the world. When asked about these numerous voice over cases, Waits replied "[The voice is] part of an artist's odyssey, discovering your own voice and struggling to find the combination of qualities that makes you unique. It's kind of like your face, your identity. Now I've got these unscrupulous doppelgängers out there - my evil twin who is undermining every move I make."

The Midler and Waits courts recognizes the value of a celebrity's voice. But how do distinguish those cases to a similar case involving strikingly similar facts involving singer, Nancy Sinatra. Arguably, the Sinatra name has been synonymous with singing for many generations. In Sinatra's situation, Goodyear produced a television commercial for their "Wide Boots" tires featuring *These Boots Are Made for Walking*, the song she made popular. Like the other cases, the song was rerecorded for the commercial with someone else's voice. Like the facts in the *Midler* case, Goodyear sought and obtained the permission of the music publisher for use of the composition. The advertisement featured an actress wearing white boots and a miniskirt, much like the signature appearance of Nancy at the height of her career in the 60's. One important distinction in this instance, however, is that the actress clearly did not bear any resemblance to Sinatra. This fact indicates that even though Goodyear used a song and costume identified with Sinatra, there was ostensibly no deliberate intent to imitate or impersonate Sinatra and, more importantly according to the court, the public was not likely deceived into thinking that Sinatra was, in fact, endorsing the product by appearing in the advertisement. This sets the case apart from the Waits and Midler situations, where the court perceived some attempt to deceive. The courts' perception is supported by the distinguishing fact that in both the Waits and the Midler cases, the artists were initially approached by the advertisers seeking their participation and were turned down, whereas here Goodyear did not approach Sinatra to appear in the advertisement.

Imitating a real person is one thing, but branding, celebrity persona, trademark, and copyright all begin to meld together when one thinks about actors portraying beloved fictional characters, superheroes, and villains: William Conrad as Matt Dillion on *Gunsmoke*, Christopher Reeves as *Superman*, Adam West as *Batman*, Clayton Moore as the *Lone Ranger*, Mark Hamill as *Luke Skywalker*, James Earl Jones as the voice of *Darth Vadar*, and Wayne Knight as *Seinfeld's* Newman. Often, the fan perceives that the actors blend with the characters they portray. In reality, these fictional characters are intellectual property belonging to a third party, usually a conglomerate. This can be problematic for the actors who get "type-cast" in that role and have difficulty obtaining other employment.

There are numerous legal implications that flow from this kind of character/actor convergence, particularly when these actors or actresses don costumes of the fictional characters as a side profession and/or routinely get paid to appear in public promoting the fictional character. Since these actors are not generally the owner of the intellectual properties embodied in the fictional characters and their body of work, the celebrity can be the subject of an infringement lawsuit.

I am not necessarily referring to the more benign occupation of many college students who dress up as a Disney princess and attend a prepubescent kid's party, but rather something a bit more confusing for the public. Most of these children's party impersonators go undetected by the owners of the intellectual property and "fly under the radar," thereby evading liability. Disney, one of the most aggressive enforcers of its intellectual property, would most certainly go after anyone who substantially reproduces or exploits its properties if they feel their intellectual property is being threatened or demeaned in any way. However, the legal departments of most conglomerates are so backlogged with ongoing caseloads to pursue such an action, or disregard the use as *de minimis*, or simply have not been made aware of the infringement.

The character imitation that presents the more interesting and threatening issue is perhaps best exemplified by the legal problems of Clayton Moore with regard to his near-delusional character imitation of the Lone Ranger. For most of us who grew up in the 50's and 60's, Moore was the Lone Ranger: the chiseled statue of a man portraying the character in television and movies from 1949 until approximately 1959, and then in syndication for years after that. Moore was and forever will be synonymous with the Ranger's exit phrase "Hi-yo Silver, away."

But in 1978, the Wrather Corporation, who owned the rights to the Lone Ranger character and produced Moore's original television series by the same name, decided to license the production of a new movie called *The Legend of the Lone Ranger*. Wrather decided to use a younger, unknown actor by the name of Klinton Spilsbury. Wrather had a serious problem, however, in that Moore, who sometimes admitted to the delusion, refused to leave his house without being decked out as the Lone Ranger, wearing western suits, cowboy hats, spurs and, of course, the black mask. So the corporation took the case to Superior Court in Los Angeles seeking an injunction to prevent Moore from appearing in public as the Lone Ranger.

The facts of this case were easy for the judge, since the Wrather Corporation definitively owned the intellectual property that is the Lone Ranger: they had every right to dictate who could and could not present themselves in public as the Lone Ranger. It was what we lawyers refer to in the profession as a legal "slam dunk." Moore was forced to wear sunglasses in place of the Lone Ranger's trademark mask.

The legal case may have been an clear fact pattern, but sometimes public opinion and backlash are at odds with slam dunk legal opinions. That is the reason criminal attorneys like to "try their cases in the media" to build support for the defendant. So when the new Lone Ranger movie opened, audiences protested and avoided it in support of Moore, their favorite Lone Ranger. The movie turned into one of the biggest box office bombs in history. The actor Klinton Spilsbury was never heard from again.

Perhaps inspired by the overwhelming outpouring of support, Moore countersued for the right to continue wearing the mask, and the case dragged on for years until it was suddenly dropped by Jack Wrather in September 1984. When Wrather dropped dead a month later, his wife sent a letter to Moore granting Moore the right to wear the Lone Ranger mask once again, which he did until his death in 1999. Hi-yo Silver, away.

The litany of examples of impersonations in this chapter illustrates how reputation and celebrity fuel the entertainment industry. The "fame" can come from brands, personas, characters, voices, attributes, and many other characteristics, all of which can blend together to give a person or a character its celebrity. And of course, a dead celebrity (or "deleb" as some call them) incorporates all of these elements as well, and can often be exploited through "post-mortem rights," something explored in the next chapter. One of the primary lessons to be learned from this chapter is that if there is value to any of these types of "fame" or "celebrity," there is a definitive legal right to protect it against activity that seeks to divert that value from the proper recipient, or confuse the public into buying a product or service that is not associated with that celebrity

Post-Mortem Rights

We all shine on...
like the moon and the stars and the sun...
we all shine on...and on and on....
-John Lennon

The Scottish poet, Thomas Campbell once said "to live in the hearts we leave behind is not to die." If any among us have achieved the immortality of which Lennon and Campbell spoke, it is the deceased celebrities whose estates have continued to feed our fantasies that "Elvis is in the house." During the 1997 Super Bowl, Dirt Devil incorporated some digital magic into a commercial that featured manipulated footage of Fred Astaire's famous hat rack dance from the movie *Royal Wedding*, replacing the rack with one of its Dirt Devil floor sweepers. The effect was a very impressive and memorable commercial. However, this digital sleight of hand angered Astaire's daughter, Robyn, who had been charged with overseeing his rights of publicity and felt strongly that the commercialization demeaned Astaire's art. "Fred left me in charge of his legacy, and I promised to oversee his creative property as he would have," Robyn said. "It's been difficult to keep my promise."[27] What ensued was years of litigation, ending in a loss for the Astaire estate in the lawsuit, but a final victory with the passage of California's SB209, the "Astaire Bill," that extended California's post-mortem rights of publicity

---

[27] Testifying in front of a California Senate Committee in regard to Senate Bill 209.

to include plays, books, magazines, films and other media, and required permission from the estate to exploit them. This raises the philosophical and legal question of whether the dead should have the same rights of publicity as the living, and be allowed to pass that along to their heirs.

As we saw earlier, the existence of rights of publicity is not uniform in the United States, and where there is variance for the living, there is exponential variance for the dead. When New York passed that first statute relating to a right of publicity in 1903, discussed earlier, there were no guidelines for such laws. The New York legislators therefore viewed publicity rights more as a *personal right*, as opposed to a property right, and therefore the right literally died with the "person" and could not be passed down to future generations. However, the line of thinking that followed the passage of that law, as well as the states that followed New York's lead and passed publicity statutes of their own, began to treat this newly recognized right as more of a *property right*, much like the other intellectual properties copyright, trademark, and patent. It follows that if the right of publicity is, in fact, a *property* right, it can be passed down to heirs like any other commodity, contrary to New York law.

Scholars soon began to recognize the importance of extending the right of publicity to the estate of the personality, because it is in fact a property right. New York has still not passed legislation to extend the right of publicity after a celebrity's death, although several bills have been before the

68

legislature in the past decade, but it is in the minority. In most states, the right of publicity became a post-mortem right which could be passed down to a celebrity's heirs just like their money, jewelry, boats, cars, houses, and other personal possessions.

If we use my earlier discussion of Roger Federer as an example of the logic here, let's assume Roger were to pass away,  God forbid. Why should his wife and their twin daughters and sons not be permitted to continue to benefit financially from his esteemed name, image, and logo in order to protect those properties from unauthorized and dilutive commercial uses? Shouldn't Roger's beautiful family be allowed to receive the revenues from the sponsorships, relationships, and other contractual rights entered into by Roger during his lifetime, as well as continue to exploit and develop other streams of income? Logically, if the right of publicity is a property right as has been argued, then the celebrity's family should benefit from his or her stream of income, just as those heirs who receive stock certificates in the company of their deceased family members and continue to receive the dividends.

The develop of postmortem rights of publicity, to date, has primarily occurred in states that have a nucleus of entertainment-related industries, where there is a significant interest in protection the rights of celebrities who died there:

Tennessee (Elvis), California (Marilyn Monroe) and Washington (Hendrix), just to name a few. Currently, most states recognize the importance of the descendability of these rights of publicity, as the statutes in most instances apply not only to the living, but also on a post-mortem, *i.e.*, after death, basis so that the family estates of the celebrity may benefit from their popularity.

Much of the legislation that currently exists is in large part the direct result of the efforts of Mark Roesler, who founded CMG Worldwide to exploit the rights of deceased celebrities such as legends James Dean and Marilyn Monroe. When Roesler graduated law school, he wanted to be an agent, but he realized that most of the living celebrities were represented by existing Hollywood agencies. He lived down the road from the relatives of James Dean, so he figured if he couldn't represent the living, it might be easier to represent the dead. So, Roesler successfully rallied behind the passage of legislation in states where his clients had died. As a result, his home state of Indiana has one of the most far-reaching rights of publicity statutes, providing recognition of the right for a period of 100 years after death and protecting not only the more common rights to the name, image, and likeness, but extending protection to a celebrity's signature, photographs, gestures, distinctive appearance, and mannerisms as well.[28] The statute also has a provision that "reaches back" 100 years to protect the rights of celebrities that died prior to its passage.

---

[28] IC 32-36-1-8.

Roseler was not the only entrepreneur that realized the value of a popular celebrity who had died. The estate of Elvis has been exploiting his phenomenon for years after his tragic death. The principle of descendability was developed, in large part, in a line of cases involving his estate. The first case to deal with the Elvis estate was in New Jersey, which, at the time, had no statute regarding post-mortem rights of publicity. In that case, *Estate of Presley v. Russen*,[29] the defendant produced a musical variety show patterned after Elvis' show called "The Big EL" show. In their advertisements, Russen frequently used various properties of the Elvis estate, including the phrase "The King," a name by which Elvis was universally known. The district court examined whether use of the phrase in the defendant's musical production was a violation of the Presley estate's inherited right of publicity, considering mostly principles derived from trademark law. The court noted that "[t]he 'right of publicity,' having been characterized by New Jersey courts as a property right, rather than as a right personal to and attached to the individual, is capable of being disassociated from the individual and transferred by him for commercial purposes."[30] Recognizing the inherent natural rights basis for this concept, the court concluded "If the right is descendible, the individual is able to transfer the benefits of his labor to his immediate successors and is assured that control over the exercise of the right can be vested in a suitable

---

[29] 513 F. Supp. 1339 (D.N.J 1981).
[30] *Id.*, at 1354.

beneficiary."[31] While it recognized the post-mortem rights, the court balanced those rights against Russen's First Amendment right and druled that Russen could continue to operate The Big El show as long as they clearly advertised that it was an *imitation* of Elvis in order to prevent "marketplace confusion."

In a handful of jurisdictions across the country, the courts will require that the exploitation of a person's rights of publicity be carried out during the lifetime of the celebrity before they will allow a cause of action for post-mortem right of publicity. This is true, for example, in Utah (*Nature's Way Prods., Inc. v. Nature-Pharma, Inc.*, 736 F.Supp. 245 (D. Utah 1990)) and Arizona (*Sinkler v. Goldsmith*, 623 F.Supp. 727 (D. Ariz. 1985)). It should be noted that the decisions reached in these cases are exceptions since the logic is drastically flawed: it is the equivalent of requiring that a stock warranty be exercised during the decedent's lifetime as a condition to allow it be passed to the heirs.[32] The majority of jurisdictions apply the principle first stated in *Russen*, that both the statutory or common law principle of rights of publicity are descendible property which has a postmortem duration not conditioned on exploitation during the person's lifetime.

---

[31] *Id.*, 1355.

[32] 2. J. Thomas McCarthy, *Rights of Publicity and Privacy*, $9:17. See, also, *Martin Luther King, Jr. Center for Social Changes, Inc. v. American Heritage Products, Inc.*, 694 F.2d 674, 678 (11th Cir. 1983), which specifically rejected the requirement of exploitation during lifetime.

Naturally, the length of protection for post-mortem rights of publicity varies from state to state. Tennessee's statute, The Personal Rights Protection Act, passed in 1984, recognizes that the right extends to the person's heirs "for a period of ten (10) years after the death of an individual."[33]   After that, it will continue for additional subsequent ten-year periods unless terminated for "non-use" if the heirs fail to exploit the rights for a continuing period of two years.   That means that, effectively, if the estate continues to exploit the rights of publicity, Tennessee post-mortem rights are indefinite.   As noted earlier, Indiana's statute has the longest established period of descendability, giving heirs not only a postmortem right of 100 years, but also the so-called "reach back" component that protects celebrities that died during the 100-year period prior to the statute. Oklahoma comes in a close second, with a 100-year post-mortem right and a 50-year reach back provision.   Close contenders include Washington (75), California (70), Texas, Kentucky and Nevada (50). Some states provide more limited rights after death, such as Florida at 40 years and Virginia, the lowest, at 20 years.

Inconsistencies among state laws regarding a particular issue will inevitably lead to litigation over that particular issue, and the postmortem rights of personality is no exception to this rule. In these kinds of cases, a critical decisive factor is where the celebrity was domiciled prior to his or her death, a fact that determines which state's law is applied to the case and whether

---

[33] T.C.A. §47-25-1104(a)

and how long the rights are protected. The New York and California statutes were at the center of just such a determination in a notable case concerning Marilyn Monroe. In the New York case of *Shaw Family Archives Ltd v CMG Worldwide, Inc*,[34] the court grappled with whether to apply New York or California law in regard to a claim filed on behalf of the estate of Marilyn Monroe by none other than Mark Roesler. The late photographer Sam Shaw had taken several images of Marilyn Monroe during his lifetime, in particular, the most famous photograph of her standing above a subway grate while her white skirt blew wildly in the wind. The photograph is certainly one of the most frequently thought of images of "Norma Rae," and has become a cult classic, inspiring Elton John's homage *Candle in the Wind.* The estate of Shaw contended that they could sell these iconic images without paying a license fee to the Monroe estate, thus pitting one type of intellectual property, the copyright in the photographs, against another, the postmortem rights of Monroe.

With regard to state citizenship, Monroe died in 1962 in California, but was also arguably a citizen of New York. Both sides mounted extensive evidence: Monroe's estate argued that Monroe was a citizen of California, which had an applicable postmortem statute, while the estate of Shaw argued in favor of New York law, which does not recognize the postmortem right. In the end, however, the court noted that where she lived was a

---

[34] 486 F Supp 2d 309 (SDNY 2007).

74

moot issue, since no matter which state's law it applied, Monroe's heirs did not inherit her rights of publicity in the photographs. With regard to the California statute favored by the estate of Monroe, the court concluded that she died before the passage of California's Celebrity Rights Act in 1985, which had no reach back provision, and therefore had no rights under that state's law. As to Shaw's argument in favor of New York law, the court reasoned that since New York does not recognize a post-mortem right of publicity, Monroe's name, image, and voice fell into the "public domain" after her death. The court concluded that either way "any publicity rights she enjoyed during her lifetime were extinguished at her death by operation of law." As a result, the estate could not have inherited any property right that Monroe did not own at the time of her death. The current implication of this ruling is that Monroe's name, image, and voice are in the public domain in any state that did not recognize a post-mortem right of publicity at the time of her death in 1962 or have a reach back provision. In response to the New York decision, California passed legislation creating a right of publicity that lasts 70 years after death (Cal Civ Code §3344.1) and, as noted, many state enacted legislation incorporating a "reach back" provision to prevent similar injustices.

In contrast to the *Shaw* opinion, the California case of *Hebrew University of Jerusalem v General Motors LLC*,[35] reached

---

[35] No CV10-03790 (CD Cal, March 16 2012).

contradictory conclusions when applying the law of New Jersey. As a member of first Board of Governors for Hebrew University, the famed physicist and mathematician Albert Einstein bequeathed over 55,000 personal papers, including the copyrights and publication rights to the university, upon his death in 1955. The bequest also included the rights to his "image" and therefore, ostensibly his rights of publicity. Hebrew University took issue with General Motors' advertisement that appeared in *People* for its 2010 terrain vehicle featuring Einstein's head superimposed onto a lingerie model's body. When GM refused to stop running the advertisement, the University sued.

One of the causes of actions in the complaint was based on California's right of publicity statute.[36] However, the court correctly observed that the California statute requires that the claim be construed using the laws of the testator's domicile at death. Since Einstein died in Princeton, the court applied New Jersey law. While New Jersey appellate courts recognize the *common law* right of publicity, the state does not have a right of publicity *statute*.[37] In response to a motion for summary judgment filed by the University, GM argued that Einstein had no post-mortem publicity rights to grant to the University because such a right did not exist in New Jersey at the time of his death. That

---

[36] (Ca Civ Code § 946).
[37] The New Jersey legislature considered passing a rights of publicity statute in 2007 and 2008, but to date it has not enacted one.

argument drew heavily from the principles expressed by the court in the *Shaw* opinion.

The court analyzed the rights of publicity extensively, recognizing that they are "akin to an intellectual property" and in that extent are descendible. Having arrived at that conclusion, the court examined the various state laws regarding the length of postmortem rights, summarized earlier in this chapter, and arrived at the conclusion that *on average*, 50 years is the length of time that most reasonably balances the rights of an estate against a person's First Amendment rights of Free Speech. According to the court, since Einstein had passed away in 1955, the Hebrew University possessed the right to exploit the rights of publicity until 2005, four years before they filed the complaint in 2009. Although it ruled against the Hebrew University in this specific regard, this decision arrived at the opposite conclusion of the *Shaw* case discussed above, primarily as a result of the court's examination of various laws of different states. The court noted that the Hebrew University always had the legal recourse of appealing to New Jersey's state legislature for a specific statute protecting its rights.

This path through the halls of the State Legislature is precisely the journey taken in Washington State in response to litigation regarding Jimi Hendrix and the subsequent passage of amendments to its 1998 Personality Rights Act. Unfortunately, this resulted in a legal battle between the state's legislative body and its court system, resulting in precedence that could have a negative impact on a descendible right of publicity nationwide. The facts of the case take us back to the death of Jimi Hendrix in London in 1970. Hendrix died intestate, meaning he died without a will and with no wife or children. As a result, Jimi's father, Al Hendrix, was the sole heir to his estate.[38]

Al Hendrix subsequently assigned his rights to the estate in 1995 to two limited liability companies, Experience Hendrix and Authentic Hendrix,[39] who, that same year, filed a complaint against a third company called Electric Hendrix, alleging violations of their newly acquired rights. A Federal District Court in Washington State dismissed the case out of hand, ruling that Hendrix was a resident of New York at the time of his death and New York's common law must apply to the case. Once again, since New York law only recognizes the right as applying to the living, there were no rights of publicity to be passed along to Al Hendrix and, therefore, he could not assign or transfer them. Hendrix appealed the decision to the Ninth Circuit, but that court agreed and affirmed the decision of the lower court.[40]

In 2008, in direct response to the Ninth Circuit decision, the Washington State House of Representatives introduced House Bill 2727 to strengthen their original Personality Rights

---

[38] . Experience Hendrix, L.L.C. v. HendrixLicensing.com, Ltd., 766 F. Supp. 2d 1122, 1127 (W.D. Wash. 2011).

[39] . *See Experience Hendrix, L.L.C. v. James Marshall Hendrix Foundation.*, No. C03-3462Z, 2005 WL 2922179, *2 (W.D. Wash. Nov. 4, 2005).

[40] . *Experience Hendrix, L.L.C. v. James Marshall Hendrix Foundation*, 240 F. App'x 739 (9th Cir. 2007)

Act[41] by including a provision that protected deceased personalities who died before 1998, thereby making it applicable to the Hendrix estate. In addition to Hendrix, it is important to realize that Washington is home to Getty Images and Corbis (owned by Bill Gates), companies concerned with licensing various aspects of post-mortem rights of publicity.[42] The amendment, passed by a majority, provided that the right of publicity continues after a person's death regardless of where the person was domiciled when they died or whether the jurisdiction where the person was domiciled recognized a similar right at the time of death, i.e., it basically instructed a court to ignore choice of law provisions when applying the statute.

Because the amended statute effectively created a national right of publicity claim for any plaintiff who was able to obtain personal jurisdiction in the state of Washington, it raised serious Constitutional issues. So when the complaint in the lower court was amended and refiled, the Washington State court that originally heard the case took it upon itself to review the Constitutionality of the new amendments to Washington's Personality Rights Act, declaring them violative of the Due Process and Full Faith and Credit Clauses, as well as the dormant Commerce Clause. It struck down the language that

---

[41]. H.B. Rep. 2727, 60th Leg., Reg. Sess., at 2 (Wash. 2008).

[42] See Phillip Barengolts, *Amending a Washington State Statute to Ignore Choice of Law Principles Could Not Gain Jimi Hendrix's Heirs a Post-Mortem Right of Publicity: Court Rules Amendment Unconstitutional*, PATISHALL IP BLO (March 31, 2011).

circumvented choice of law principles. Similar constitutional arguments may be levied against the aforementioned "reach back" provisions in other states' laws. The court's opinion here is legally correct in terms of constitutionality, but the precedent produces a grossly unfair consequence for post-mortem rights of publicity.

Fact patterns such as *Hendrix* point to the very real need for a federal right of publicity statute that would provide one clear and consistent standard for publicity rights throughout the country and resolve the patchwork of inconsistent court opinions and statutes concerning postmortem descendability. This amalgam of state laws and statutes create confusing and disparate results. This not only raises the costs of litigation, it also increases the costs of marketing and licensing efforts by rights holders. Again, this stresses the need for a federal statute to harmonize state laws and provide predictability in this important area.

Celebrity Branding & Trademark Development

From the day you're born, you're branding yourself as one thing or another.

-Daymond John, *The Brand Within*

Up until now, we have been primarily considering the impact a celebrity can make on a particular product or brand by licensing their fame for purposes of endorsement. There is, however, another important component of the overall branding picture that plays a significant role, and that is branding a product through the effective use of image and trademark, then connecting it to your celebrity endorser's values and believes. My client, Daymond John, in his book *The Brand Within*, observed that during Barrack Obama's first "Yes we Can" presidential campaign, when the ubiquitous "O" started appearing on car bumpers, windows and in front yards everywhere, the cola company Pepsi coincidentally changed its logo to incorporate a similarly designed "O" around its traditional patriotic colors of red, white and blue. Was that just serendipity, or was Pepsi seizing an opportunity to capitalize on a national movement and cash in on its success? When it comes to brands and competitive marketing, there are no accidents.

Just as a celebrity has an image and persona, so too does a brand. Remember the "blue pinstripe" IBM letters that served as its logo throughout the 70's. At the ti me, it was intended to convey the image of a well-dressed business person. IBM reinforced this connection by promoting a

corporate culture that encouraged their employees to wear pinstripe suits with pale blue dress shirts. We have already discussed Apple's simple logo, the silhouette of an apple with a bite taken out, that conveys a Zen-like simplicity of design, one of the hallmarks of Apple's corporate image. A company's choice of a logo or brand, which is subsequently trademarked, is one of the most important aspects of their success.

While some believe these types of commercial logos and trademarks emblazoned on goods and services is a byproduct of our current age of extreme commercialization, the practice actually dates

back to the Roman Empire. As early as 500 B.C.E., the swordsmiths would imprint their unique symbol on their swords to denote not only its source, but as a symbol of quality and distinction. They wanted their "consumers" to know who had made this fine instrument of battle. Swords of the best blacksmiths were highly sought after and cherished, much in the same way as consumers search for particular products today.

The industry of selling alcoholic beverages has always been efficient with their branding and marketing efforts. The craft of brewing beer, which dates back to the Dark Ages, has a long history of associating an "image" with its finely crafted beverages in order to convey certain messages about the product, often using a series of one to three x's to denote the strength of the brew. Just before and during the Renaissance, about the 13th Century, hops became a very common ingredient in beers, especially in northern Europe, because of its attributes, which both flavored and preserved the final product.[43] For this reason, beer

trademarks are some of the oldest continuously-used trademarks in existence. For example, the brewing of Stella Artois dates back to 1366, an "anno" that is proudly exhibited in its logo. The chronicles of the city of Leuven, Belgium show that its original brewer, the "Den Hoorn" brewery, regularly paid their taxes. Den Hoorn was later sold to Sebastien Artois.

Similarly, Löwenbräu is said to have been founded around 1383, once again proudly emblazoned on its logo, which

---

[43] Wilson, C. Anne. Food and Drink in Britain from the Stone Age to the 19th Century. Chicago: Academy Chicago Publishers, 1991, p. 375.

features the lion emblem that was carved into the fresco of the brewery, ostensibly depicting the Biblical story of Daniel in the lion's den.

In England, the Bass Brewery, founded in 1777 by William Bass, began producing a variety of ales, including its popular pale ale. Bass is said to be a pioneer in the field of international brand marketing as one of the first breweries to take advantage of formal trademark registration. In 1875, the United Kingdom passed the Trademark Registration Act, which became effective on January 1, 1876. The Bass Brewery claims titles to the first two trademark registrations under that Act: the Bass Red Triangle for their pale ale, which is most familiar today, and the Bass Red Diamond for their strong ale. The fame of Bass' Red Triangle logo has been immortalized, appearing in art and literature. For example, Édouard

Manet's 1882 painting *A Bar at the Folies-Bergère* incorporates the mark[44] as do over 40 paintings by Picasso at the height of his Cubist period. James Joyce, skilled weaves it into the "Oxen of the Sun" episode of *Ulysses*, when the character Bloom observes

---

[44]Bendiner, Kenneth. *Food in painting: from the Renaissance to the present.* Reaktion Books, 2004, page 73.

the "number one" Bass logo.[45] A brand that can penetrate into cultural references to this depth, the associated product will be around for many generations.

All three of these logos for these traditional beers instantly convey to the consumer that the brewery are part of a long lineage, but they also, in various ways, convey strength, stability and royalty. Like the celebrities used to endorse a company's products and brand, a well designed logo can immediately convey distinct impressions to the consumer about the quality and content of the product. A company strives to build not only brand awareness, but also association, awareness, and loyalty, as illustrated in the following diagram:

[45]"During the past four minutes or thereabouts he had been staring hard at a certain amount of number one Bass bottled by Messrs. Bass and Co at Burton-on-Trent which happened to be situated amongst a lot of others right opposite to where he was and which was certainly calculated to attract anyone's remark on account of its scarlet appearance." — Episode XIV, Ulysses, James Joyce (1922).

Some companies spend millions of dollars hiring consultatnts, graphic artists, design firms, and advertising firms in order to design the perfect logo to identify their brands. One of the most legendery examples of this process is the FedEx trademark created in 1994. When he created the FedEx logo, design artist Lindon Leader was inspired by the idea of using of negative white

space in order to veil hidden meaning. The old Bank of America logo was one of his favorite examples, using the negative white space forming the "b" and "a" to convey the image of an America eagle. That inspiration gave Linden his "first 'aha' into what design needs to be: "Simple and Clear." So Linden set about with that concept when he designed the now iconic FedEx logo. Fred Smith, the CEO of FedEx, was a saavy client with obvious design and marketing skills of his own. Although he had built Federal Express, as it was called then, into a massive global presence, people still thought of them as primarily a U.S. company with limited overnight package delivery services. He wanted to expand that image. Smith wanted new graphic designs and didn't care if the company need a brand image makeover. "My trucks are moving billboards," Smith told Linden, "I better be able to see a FedEx truck loud and clear from five blocks away." Tasked with the goal of rebranding the company, Linden set about to design a new logo and brand. Drawing from the Bank of America logo, he used the negative white space between the orange "E" and "x" to create an arrow and subtlely convey the idea that FedEx was moving " in a forward direction" with "speed and precision." If the arrow remained hidden in the white space, it gave that idea with power and an element of surprise. "Undestatement is much more elegant," says Linden.[46] Since its creation, the FedEx logo has garnered over forty design awards and been identified as one of the top ten logos in the last four decades by *Rolling*  *Stones* magazine. Apple took this design concept of "simple and clear" to the extreme in 2006, emblazoning the lids to its popular PowerBook and MacBook computers with it logo literally glowing in the negative white space from by the surrounding solid colored casing.

While saavy companies know the power of a well-designed trademark, the truly exceptional ones know that combining that impact with the strenght of a well thought out celebrity alliance is potent. One of the more successful companies to combine the two strengths over the years is Nike. Nike's legendery "Swoosh" logo also uses the concept of "simple and clear," but Nike's real success is in its use of athletic celebrities to help build a brand. In doing so, they have built a corporate image that conveys that it is THE brand used by the highest level

---

[46] May, Matthew. "The Story behind the Famous FedEx Logo, and why it Works." Fast Company. Excerpt from May's book, *The Laws of Subtraction*. McGraw-Hill. 2012.

achievers, the winners, which in turn reflects its corporate values of achievement, performance, and innovation. They look for celebrities that have the same personality and values as their brand and company. Nike has masterfully capitalized on America's idolized view of athletes as heroes to build an equal image in the mind of its target market, the young and viral.

There is no better example of this than Nike's relationship with basketball legend Michael Jordan. In the early 1980's, the big name in athletic shoes was Converse. When he played for North Carolina, Jordan wore Converse because his

coach, Dean Smith, was getting paid to have his players wear them. Jordan's preference was Adidas. So when Jordan graduated, he was being courted by all the greats shoe manufacturers to wear their products in the NBA, including Adidas and Converse, but he also caught the eye of a fairly unknown little shoe manufacturer, at the time, called Nike. Nike was a young company at the time, and they really wanted an rising star on whose tail they ride. In the end, neither Adidas nor Converse could match Nike's final offer to Jordan, $500,000 a year for five years plus royalties. Ultimately Jordan decided to wear a brand of shoes he had never worn before. The first "Air Jordan" basketball shoes were produced in 1984 and the rest is history. Advertisements for the shoes featured Jordan jumping to dunk

the basketball. The shoes sold so well, that it wasn't too long before Nike became a household name and offered Jordan a partnership for more than just shoes. For that partnership, they developed a new logo, a silhouette form in the shape of the "Jumpman" himself, Jordan, patterned after the photograph seen on the prior page. The brand is owned by a collaborative effort between Jordan and Nike, a subsidiary of Nike known as the Jordan Brand. The Jumpman is now recognized internationally. In 2013, sales of footware, hoodies, shorts, and apparrel featuring the new logo, generated $3.2 billion in  profits, contributing a signifacant percentage of Nike's overall revenue of $26 billion. Jordan Brand recently opened a MJ specific Nike story outside of Madison Square Garden. Now, Michael Jordan receives approximately 45-50% of the net profits of the Jordan Brand. He is the "perfect athlete" for Nike, and the Jumpman is the perfect brand for their alliance.[47]

A powerful and defining association between a celebrity and a brand such as the success of the Jumpman is something that can be repeated in many diverse industries. In 2001, Busta

---

[47] Badenhausen, Kurt. "How Michael Jordan Made $90 Million in 2013." Forbes. February 27, 2014. As a quick aside, the original photographer of the "Jumpman" picture from which the trademark was derived, Jacobus Rentmeester, recently sued the company in an Oregon court for copyright infringement, claiming that the company created a derivative work without his permission.

Rhymes released his hit single *Pass the Courvoisier*, without a branding deal in place with the manufacturer of the infamous cognac, Beam Suntory, yet the company's sales increased 30% in the United States in the months following the release. The impact that the lyrical reference to a product made on sales of that prdouct was not lost on the music industry, and soon joint ventures deals begin to form directly between manufacturers and artists to promote specific products through the artists' teams. One recent example of such a collaboration is the endorsement deal that Diageo liquors struck with The Blue Fame Agency for the services of Sean Combs ("Puff Daddy" or "Diddy"). Prior to the deal, in 2007, the London-based Diageo's vodka brand, Cîroc, was struggling in the market, selling a paltry 40,000 cases a year. Although it was distilled from French grapes instead of potatoes or corn, the premium vodka was pratically unknown outside of Diageo itself. Combs' agent convinced Diageo that they could promote the superior quality of Cîroc by selling the concept of a "lifestyle" brand to Combs' social networks and fan bases. Combs agreed to take on the responsibility of building the brand and selling it to his fans in exchange for a 50% partnership. Through viral video campaigns and daily posts on social media, Combs continues to promote the brand. As of December 2012, the joint venture had reportedly sold over 2.1 million cases of the vodka, and the value of the brand has increased to a cool $1 billion, making Diddy a very rich man and Cîroc a household name.

Since the success of the Cîroc deal, similar deals were struck by various celebrities, including actors, dancers, musicians and atheletes: Jay Z (Armand de Brignac Champagne and D'usse Cognac), Dan Aykroyd (Crystal Head Vodka), Sammy Hagar (Cabo Wabo Tequila), Joe Montana (Aviation Gin), Justin Timberlake (901 Silver Tequila), George Clooney (Casamigos Tequila), Ludacris (Conjure Cognac), Kenny Chesney (Blue Chair Bay Rum), CeeLo Green (Ty Ku Sake), and the unlikely duo of Bill Murray and Mikhail Baryshnikov (Slovenia Vodka).

A method that works for fine liquor will most likely work for fine food as well. Another area of entertainment where this concept of branding fame generates massive income is in the niche arena of celebrity chefs. The success stories of such icons as Wolfgang Puck, Emeril Lagasse, Rachel Ray, and other foodies are stunningly similar to the aforemention sports figures and entertainers, except in this case it is usually the chefs that are the unknowns prior to exploiting their craft in other areas.

In the late 80's, Wolfgang Puck's California restaurant, Spago, caused a local consumer sensation, propelling Puck into instant stardom. Chef Puck leveraged that local, albeit extensive, reputation by aggressively opening more restaurants and related businesses. The Puck global brand exploded internationally and now includes fast-casual Wolfgang Puck Gourmet Express restaurants in the United States, Canada, and Japan, as well as branded cookware, utensils and appliances, and a complete line of frozen and packaged foods that includes pizza, soups, and

91

coffee. A similar path to success was taken by Cajun Chef Emeril Lagasse, known to the world as "Emeril." His trademark "BAM" expression when spicing a dish has become a household expression during dinner preparations across America. A simple New Orleans restauranteur in 1990, he has created a worldwide phenomenon in Cajun cooking and now runs eleven restaurants, has authored twelve cookbooks, hosted numerous successful television shows, and does celebrity endorsements for such non-related products as Crest toothpaste. Like many of the chefs in this list, Emeril is, in fact, now more of an entertainment commodity than a chef. His co-ventures include a line of cookware, "Emerilware," which features cast iron skillets, cutlery, fryers, grills, and steamers. Lagasse also sells tableware, a full line of kitchen and casual apparel, and even cooking music. Of couse, he also has a food brand that includes signature coffees, cooking spray, spices, sauces, salsas, salad dressings, marinades, and mustards. In February 2008, Emeril Lagasse's non-restaurant holdings were purchased by Martha Stewart Living Omnimedia at an estimated cost of $50 million.[48] Similar statistics abound for niche celebrities, like *Good Eats* star Alton Brown, who introduced the world to the science of cooking and then proceeded to become the face of the Food Network, hosting other cooking shows with his quick witted commentary.

---

[48] Silversten, Barry. "Brands that cook in the kitchen." Brandchannel.com, May 5, 2008.

Rachel Ray, another chef phenom, leveraged her celebrity to become a commenatator in non-food-related ventures. She first came to the nation's attention in 2002 as the host of Food Network's mid-market cable series *$40 a Day*, in which she toured America to show how to dine in its favorites cities on a $40 budget. Ray has the expected lineup of food-related products just like all the other chefs, including cookware, food products and even her line of pet food, "Nutrish." But what makes Rachel different is that her success has crossed over from food shows and products into mainstream medias and general entertainment. She not only has a food and lifestyle magazine, *Every Day with Rachel Ray*, but in 2005 she collaborated with billionaire celebrity Oprah Winfrey to create a self-titled talk show which won a Daytime Emmy Award in 2008 for Outstanding Talk Show Entertainment. Going further than the other examples, Rachel Ray and her team have exploited her fame derived in the arena of cooking and turned her into a global branding phenomenon.

Puck, Lagassee, Brown and Ray helped propel the Food Network and other similar cable networks to a level of celebrity on their own, making them very successful. This principal of food related endorsement is a unique area of exploitation that can be utilzied by celebrities who are not even chefs. For example, Maria Sharapova, the aforementioned tennis champion, recently introduced a line of candies called "Sugarpova." But the celebrity who has perhaps had the most success in this arena was actor Paul Newman, whose "Newman's Own" brand venture with his friend and lawyer A.E. Hotchner, has generated hundreds of millions in sales since its inception in 1982. The venture started with "homemade" salad

dressing, and then expanded into a full line of food products including pizza sauce, frozen pizzas, lemonade, fruit cocktail juices, popcorn, salsa, grape juice, and pet foods. Each label incorporates a humerous picture of Newman dressed in a different costume to represent the product. All of the profits from the sale of his product are donated to charity through the non-profit Newman's Own Foundation. In 1993, building off the success of the brand, Newman's daughter Nell founded "Newman's Own Organics," a division of the original company that spun off in 2001 to produce healthier alternatives.

These illustrations lead to the inevitable conclusion that the realm of celebrity licensing and endorsement is expanding, and conglomerates are beginning to realize that to stand out in a crowd they must connect with the consumers by exploiting their favorites celebrities and create a singulartiy with their fan bases. Celebrities and their reprentatives, be they agents, managers, or lawyers, are well aware of the value of a powerful trademarks in that quest, particularly when combined when the power of a celebrity's well-earned reputation and popularity. They are also very aware of the power of partnering with a growing business to build a brand. This is an equally attractive commodity to a company whose goal is to build a brand and expand the awareness and sale of a product, just as Nike did with Jordan. If the core values of a celebrity's target demographic are in alignment with those of the brand, the company can easily tap into the celebrity's fan base and influence in social media, propel a new or lackluster brand, or create an international phenomenon. As we all learned from the Jumpman, "Just Do It" is the new mantra.

Measuring the Impact

Good name in man and woman, dear my lord,
Is the immediate jewel of their souls.
Who steals my purse steals trash,...
But he that filches from me my good name
Robs me of that which not enriches him,
And makes me poor indeed.

Shakespeare, *Othello*, Act III, Scene 3.

The message in the Bard's verse here is that the measure of a person is her name, or in the case of a celebrity, we might add, her fame. More precisely, for our purposes in this chapter, we explore the question of how to measure or quantify one's fame and reputation. We explored earlier how licensing the use of celebrities in advertising and/or to endorse products has grown into a multi-billion-dollar niche industry. One advertising agency estimated that companies spend almost a trillion dollars on celebrity endorsements, advertising, and social and digital media in 2011.[49] To put that in perspective, advertisers spent almost six percent of the gross national product in 2011 on celebrity endorsement or roughly $3000 per every U.S. citizen. Those numbers are astounding. When large companies spend that kind

---

[49] Shayon, Sheila. "Celebrity Endorsements is a Mixed Blessing." Brandchannel.com, Posted Feb. 9, 2011. Ad.ly spokesperson Arnie Gullov-Sing estimated that $50 billion was spent on endorsements will $35 billion was spent on digital advertising.

of money on celebrity endorsements, they go to great lengths in selecting a celebrity that will generate the most consumer interest in their product. How do they do that with any degree of accuracy? A company with a unique product to sell needs relevant information about how consumers respond to the celebrity in order to select the right fit for their marketing campaign. Using Plato's terminology from *The Rhetoric*, they need a celebrity whose *ethos* and *pathos* is aligned with the company's product image, as well as their *logos*.

Once the "Mad Men" of Madison Avenue and advertisement agencies everywhere realized that they could sell more of their clients' products by using celebrities and other notable public figures to endorse their products, it was just a matter of time one of them developed the analytics to measure fame, familiarity, and market appeal, particularly in the specific demographic to which they were trying to sell their products.

The first wave of measurement began with a man by the name of Arthur C. Nielsen, an electrical engineer and tennis champion from Chicago who pioneered the field of market research and introduced the world to the "Nielsen Ratings "and "Sweeps Week," methodologies that are still used to measure the audience appeal of television programming. Nielsen's company, ACNielsen Co., was founded in 1923 to exploit new methods of statistical sampling for purposes of determining market share and test marketing products to determine their viability. While this feat may seem commonplace in today's brand-driven society, it must be remembered that Nielsen's achievements were accomplished long before the advent of digital networks in the 1990's, which made collection of social data much simpler. Nielsen used old-fashioned "face time" to accomplish his statistical modeling, relying on random samples taken in grocery stores and retail outlets all done with a clipboard and a pencil.

Nielsen foresaw the potential in the burgeoning radio industry, the first broadcast of which had begun in 1920. By the time ACNielsen Co. developed its "National Radio Index" in the early 40's, RCA was well on its way to becoming a leader in the field. Radio, much like its distant cousin television, relied heavily on sponsors and advertising for its revenue, since there was no way to charge the consumer directly for the broadcast. Nielsen met the needs of both broadcasters and advertisers by providing them with information such as what "share" or percentage of an audience was tuned to a particular program at a particular time as well as the specific demographic breakdown of that share (*i.e.*, the age, gender, race, economic class, and geographic area). The programming was also compared on the basis of "ratings" points, *i.e.*, which show is more popular.

When radio listeners began making the transition to television viewers in 1950, Nielsen's methods were easily transferable to the new media. Likewise, all of the major players in the radio industry began converting their radio shows to television programming and continued to rely on the existing revenue model of sponsorships and paid advertisers. This revenue model increasingly required the advanced skills of Nielsen to convince advertisers to spend the money necessary to persuade viewers to purchase the advertiser's products. If a particularly popular show, such as *Friends* in the 90's, had a higher ratings point than other sitcoms, the rates charged for 30 seconds of airtime could be triple or even quadruple that charged by the less popular programming.

But knowing how many people of a certain age group watch a particularly popular program, while extremely valuable, is only half of the equation. An advertiser also wants to know if a particular celebrity, perhaps the lead actor in that program, is well liked and capable of persuading the consumer to purchase its product. After all, that is the point of advertising on the most popular programs. The reason the Super Bowl can command its high-ticket advertising dollars is because it almost always garners the highest ratings share of any programming. So, if an advertiser can persuade Peyton Manning, for example, to advertise their brand of pizza during the Super Bowl, then that particular company is likely to sell the most pizza *if* Peyton Manning is liked by a large percentage of the audience viewing the Super Bowl. This additional component to our equation indicated the need for metrics in additional to the Nielson ratings in order to allow the advertiser to weigh the value of hiring a celebrity to endorse its product.

This need for additional measurement led to the formation of another metric in 1963 called the "Q Score." Named for the "quotient" that is the result of its calculations, the Q Score, also known as the Q Rating, Q Factor, or simply the "Q," was developed by Jack Landis and is owned by the company he formed in 1964 called Marketing Evaluations, Inc. The sole purpose of the Q Score is to identify and quantify the "familiarity" of a celebrity or athlete (whether dead or alive), brand, cartoon, or some other type of entertainment commodity. By doing this, the company claimed that its Q Score is more valuable to an advertiser than how highly rated a program is because it reveals how consumers *feel* about the particular person or thing being evaluated.

Marketing Evaluations determines this "feeling" by asking the consumer a very simple question, such as "who is your favorite television actor?" Given their response, the consumer is then asked to rank similar celebrities as "one of my favorites," very good, good, fair, poor, or "never heard of." After polling a representative sample of the target population using these questions, the quotient is calculated by dividing the percentage of respondents who answered that the celebrity was one of their favorites by the total percentage of respondents who are familiar with that same celebrity (the sum of the remaining categories), and then multiplying that by a factor of 100. Q Scores are calculated both for the population as a whole and as to the various demographic factors of age, educational level, gender, marital status, income, etc. Further, Marketing Evaluations calculates scores based on eight categories: brand attachment, cable programming, cartoons, dead celebrities, kid's products, performers, sports figures, and television programming.

Using the Q Score, rather than just knowing how many of the viewers were tuned to a particular program, the advertiser could now determine not only how many of those viewers deemed the program to be "one of their favorite," but whether the celebrities featured in the program were among the favorite celebrities of those viewers. This combination of the Q Score with the Nielson Rating is powerful information for Kellogg's determination of whether to enter into a product placement agreement with Seinfeld to locate boxes of Corn Flakes and Shredded Wheat in Jerry's kitchen shelves. If the program *Seinfeld* has a good Nielsen Rating, is one of the most popular sitcoms among viewers, that's a good thing; but if over 50% of those viewers identify Jerry Seinfeld as one of their favorite actors or comedians, then Kellogg's can be sure the endorsement money they spend on product placement is money well spent. As you can see, the Q Score allows for that higher degree of refinement in the analysis.

The highest Q Score ever achieved by a celebrity, dead or alive, was by Bill Cosby in 1986 at the height of his career. *The Cosby Show* had one of the highest Nielsen Ratings and, of course, this allowed Cosby to score huge endorsement deals with Ford, Coca-Cola, Kodak, and, last but not least, Jell-O Pudding. "What we witnessed in the 80's with *The Cosby Show* is the perfect storm of great TV writing, a real likeable star in Bill Cosby, and wide audience appeal - the likes of which we probably will not see again," said Steve Levitt, president of Marketing Evaluations. As a point of reference, Tom Hank's Q Score in 2001 peaked at 61, while Albert Einstein, perhaps the most celebrated figure of all time, peaked at around 50. Now, with the Internet and other media options bombarding consumers for attention, "such record-breaking Q Scores are likely to be impossible to achieve."

The first real competitor to the Q Score appeared on the scene in 2006 in the form of the Davie-Brown index, created by Sharp Analytics, now marketed by the "consumer engagement" agency, The Marketing Arm, a subsidiary of Omnicom Group. Through the magic of the World Wide Web, this metric established a 1.5 million consumer research panel to evaluate how to assist advertisers in determining a celebrity's ability to influence brand affinity and the consumer's intent to purchase, introducing yet additional elements into the celebrity endorsement equation. Claiming to be more comprehensive than the Q, the DBI quantifies consumer perceptions of more than 5,000 celebrities, including TV and film stars, musical artists, reality TV stars, news personalities, politicians, athletes, and business leaders on data points such as a whether a celebrity is a breakthrough or trendsetter, and whether they exhibit trust and influence over the consumer.[50] The DBI index attempts to be more extensive in breath and content than the Q Score.

---

[50]Duff McDonald. "The Celebrity Trust Index," *New York* magazine (reposted on nymag.com), Mar 6, 2006.

Charles Dundas, the head of their strategic product innovation in London, described the DBI's market advantage this way: "Awareness is the chief criteria in determining the DBI score, but we track seven additional attributes to create a comprehensive view of a celebrity: appeal, breakthrough, trendsetter, influence, trust, endorsement and aspiration. People answer a list of questions on a [scale of one to 10] – obviously if people aren't aware of the person in question, that's it, they're out and the survey ends."[51] Using its ostensibly broader metrics, the DBI index claims to help marketers select celebrities who are more engaging and appealing to the target consumer.

Metrics such as the Q Score and the DBI may help an advertiser narrow down the field of potential candidates for an endorsement campaign, but the company must nevertheless still choose which of the multiple qualified celebrities will best identify with its consumers from the qualified pool. In other words, we may be able to determine a pool of candidates using the indices just described, but the question still remains as to how a company determines which one of those candidates is its best spokesperson. Which one will align with the consumer's tastes and interests? How did EA Sports determine that John Madden was the most effective celebrity coach or athlete to endorse its video football game? That choice may seem obvious, but it is far from it, as witnessed by the remarkable success that franchise has

---

[51] Cushman, David. "The scores are in: How our athletes fare on Rupucom's DBI Index," SportsProMedia.com, Posted May 19, 2014.

spawned. The same could be asked about George Forman's association with the griddle that bears his name, almost so synonymous that younger generations do not even realize he was a World Champion boxer before becoming the George Forman Grill. Highly successful campaigns such as these are not an accident. Once the company has acquired the necessary data on its pool of candidates using the metrics described above, it needs some means of aligning those celebrities with its desired market.

In order to answer the question of which celebrity aligns best with a company and its products, analysts and researchers have developed an equally diverse group of methodologies a company can use to evaluate and predict the success of a particular celebrity in an endorsement campaign. The granddaddy of these is the "T.E.A.R.S." method developed by T.A. Shimp in 2000.[52] Shimp simplified the process by identifying two primary attributes a company should look for in a celebrity: *credibility and attractiveness*. These two characteristics align roughly with Plato's *ethos* and *pathos* alluded to at the beginning of the chapter. Shimp maintains that these two attributes will determine the effectiveness of a celebrity's endorsement and help predict how a consumer will receive the campaign.

Shimp further divides these two categories into subcategories. With regard to credibility, a consumer will

---

[52] 41.   Shimp, T.A., *Advertising, Promotion: Supplemental aspects of Integrated Marketing Communications.* Dryden Publishers, Fort Worth, Texas. 5th Ed., 2000.

examine a celebrity's *trustworthiness* and reliability, as well as her explicit skills, or *expertise* in the particular field. These feelings the consumer has for the celebrity are then transferred to the product or brand. As for attractiveness, Shimp explains that consumers will focus not only on the *physical attractiveness* of the celebrity, but also will consider how much *respect* they have for the celebrity as well as how *similar* they perceive the celebrity to be to themselves in personality. This rounds out the acronym for the T.E.A.R.S. method: Trustworthiness, Expertise, Attractiveness, Respect and Similarity, as illustrated in the following chart:

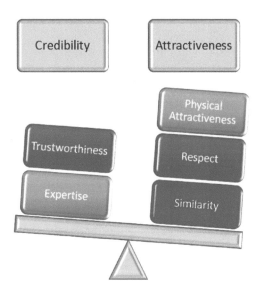

The T.E.A.R.S. Method

Shimp believes that his methodology can "identify how brand managers and their agencies actually go about selecting celebrities, as to avoid the grief from making an unwise decision." This methodology could be illustrated with many successful advertisement campaigns, but one of the most illuminating is Canon's choice of Maria Sharapova for its line of compact cameras that appeared in 2008. Sharapova is a formidable tennis champion known for being a powerful shot maker on the court. She is also respected for her physical abilities as well as her obvious attractiveness. So, when Canon went looking for a celebrity spokesperson for its "PowerShot" line of cameras, it had to determine whether her endorsement would be met with the ultimate consumer effective, sales.

Let's examine how the company may have applied using a T.E.A.R.S. analysis. Two of the attributes - physical attractiveness and expertise - were met handily: as indicated, Maria is well known as a powerful shot maker and there is no doubt as to her attractiveness. So Canon needed only to determine if Maria was a trustworthy advocate who was respected in the community. Around this time, Sharapova was coming off some significant career achievements. A few years prior, in a "break out" performance, she won the 2006 U.S. Open by defeating one of the premier players in history, Justine Henin. Sharapova spent most of the following year, 2007, atop the women's tennis charts, regaining the World No. 1 spot after a defeat to Serena Williams early in the year. She sustained an injury in the latter part of 2007, losing the French Open to Ana Ivanovic, but she made a triumphant return at the beginning of

2008, winning the Australian Open over Ivanovic to regain World No. 1 again. Sharapova was literally at the top of her sport.

The point is that Sharapova had earned the respect of her fans, who viewed her as a trustworthy and sympathetic spokesperson. The real problem for Canon was that while fans trusted her, most did not view themselves as "similar" to Sharapova. In a brilliant moment of insight, Canon's marketing team developed commercials featuring Sharapova with her Pomeranian puppy, something that makes her seem less like a superstar and more like everyone else. The story line in the commercials was that adoring fans would approach Sharapova and ask to take a picture with the PowerShot camera in their hand, to which she would respond "of course," obviously thinking the fan wanted to pose with her. But then the fan would focus in on the puppy and take a photograph, to which Maria would respond with something like "I'm right here!" Using this very clever and humorous twist, Canon's PowerShot became one of the most popular and best-selling cameras in the company's history.

As successful as the T.E.A.R.S. method may be in helping a company determine the right celebrity for a particular campaign, it fails to address other real and practical considerations that inevitably affect a company's decision to hire a celebrity. One example is cost: how much will the celebrity want for the endorsement? This significant factor is not considered when using the T.E.A.R.S. method alone. Shimp recognized this and developed a coordinate methodology which he comically called the "No TEARS" method. This method still relies on the celebrity's credibility as one of the primary factors, but introduces several other interrelated considerations as well, as can be seen in the pie chart below:

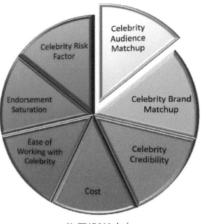

No TEARS Method

In today's competitive environment, the "risk factor" of a celebrity identified in the No TEARS method is a timely and important consideration when a company is selecting a celebrity to endorse its product or brand. The old idiom that "any publicity is good publicity" is not accurate when it comes to associating with a celebrity that falls from grace. Take Tiger Woods for example: prior to his well-publicized affair with New York city night club hostess, Rachel Uchitel, Woods had drawn in over $1 billion in all time earnings from endorsements with companies like Buick, Tag Heuer, Accenture, Gillette, AT&T, Gatorade, and, of course, Nike. After his indiscretion was revealed, however, all of his sponsors and endorsement deals vanished, except for Nike.

It is estimated that he lost close to $30 million in endorsement fees.[53]   Family-oriented companies such as Buick, AT&T, and Gillette simply cannot afford to have the reputation of their products associated with such contra-family behavior and publicity. A similar fate was bestowed on Bill Cosby, despite his Q Score, as a result of multiple revelations about his alleged sexual misconduct and indiscretions.

An additional factor introduced by the No TEARS method is the celebrity's *endorsement saturation* in the marketplace. When a person thinks of Peyton Manning, they think of what a great quarterback he is, perhaps the best in history. But think for a moment about the commercial spots you've seen featuring the great quarterback. Can you identify the product or brand Manning endorsed? Considering Manning in the context of endorsements might create confusion as to what product he endorses, because he does so many endorsements.   Is it Nationwide, Papa John's, Nabisco, Oreos, Nerf, Reebok, Gatorade, Sprint, Xbox, DirecTV, Buick, or MasterCard, among others? One might say that the only pass Manning cannot make is an endorsement! Manning is an example of endorsement saturation because his multiple appearances in dozens of commercials featuring a plethora of products tends to dilute his effectiveness in selling a singular brand or product. The No

---

[53] Rovell, Darren. "Tiger Woods' lost endorsement cost IMG $4.6M." USA Today, June 21, 2010.

TEARS method attempts to introduce this new factor as a part of the equation.

Another invaluable exercise introduced by the No TEARS metric is *aligning the celebrity with the intended market for the endorsed product brand*. The example of Manning's endorsement of Papa John's pizza is a positive illustration of this principle. On Super Bowl Sunday, a typical pizza franchise will see a 42% increase over a typical Sunday game, indicating clearly that football fans also happen to be fans of pizza. Stated in analytical terms, the demographic for Manning aligns with that of pizza. So, Papa John's really did not need either Manning's DBI or a Q Score to know that his endorsement would help generate more sales, since anyone who is a fan of Manning would be swayed by his endorsement to order their favorite pie.

One final factor introduced as an additional component of analysis by the No TEARS method is the *difficulty of working with a celebrity*. Many actors and actresses gain the reputation for being difficult to work with, and in our Internet age of instant information, knowing the difficult seeds is not neuroscience. Who can forget the emotional antics of Charlie Sheen when his producer, Chuck Lorre, fired him from the sitcom *Two and a Half Men* after eight years on the highly successful program? Highly accomplished NFL running back Terrell "T.O." Owens was notoriously difficult to be around, which ultimately led to his dismissal from almost every team with which he was associated.

Likewise, Mariah Carey was notorious for being difficult to work with during her one-year stint as a judge on *American Idol*, and the same could be said for her fellow judge, Nikki Minaj, with whom she often feuded bitterly creating awkward moments for their fellow judges. Rumors of allegedly being difficult circulate around many great actors, such as Gwyneth Paltrow, Russell Crowe, Sharon Stone, Bruce Willis, Lindsey Lohan, Steven Seagal, Kanye West, and James Cameron.

Some say this is a natural by-product of the high demands of a celebrity's careers which create stress by applying pressure for high achievement and expectations. However, this explanation does not account for the many celebrities that are a complete contrast and are reputably a "joy" to work with. This is why this final factor of the No TEARS method becomes important: for an advertiser who is spending millions of dollars to develop a marketing campaign around a celebrity, it would be irresponsible to hire a narcissistic person who makes outrageous demands and will likely run the cost of production well over budget. This consideration should not be overlooked in the evaluation.

These additional elements uncovered in the No TEARS method have led others to develop increasingly more detailed methodologies for analyzing a choice of celebrity, as illustrated by the final example, the so-called "14 Point" Method. Developed by Neha Taleja in 2010, this evaluation process incorporates elements from both the T.E.A.R.S. and No TEARS methodologies and amalgamates them into a cumulative 14-point scale, as follows:[54]

Celebrity
Credibility

Celebrity
Profession

Fit with Ad
Concept

Physical
Attractivenes
s

Celebrity Use
of Brand

Celebrity
Values

Multiple
Endorsement

Celebrity
Availability

Controversy
Risk

Cost of
Celebrity

Regional
Appeal

Celebrity
Product
Match

Target
Audience
Match

Celebrity
Popularity

14 Point Method

The goal behind the 14-Point method was to develop a "360-degree brand stewardship" that has unlimited points of contact with the intended audience. The methodology uses a basic "two attribute" system similar to the T.E.A.R.S. method (attractiveness and credibility), but instead of attractiveness substitutes the attribute of "popularity" alongside credibility. This method introduces new factors not included in the previous methodologies, such as how the celebrity *fits with the advertisement*

<hr>

[54] Taleja, Neha. "Impact of Celebrity Endorsements on Overall Brand," coolavenues.com, June 14, 2010.

concept, how much *regional appeal* does the celebrity have, and *does the celebrity utilize the brand*. Each of the 12 supporting factors, when weighed in favor of the celebrity, moves the needle up the scale from popularity to credibility, like a thermometer. Thus, if a celebrity meets nine of the factors, his score climbs to eleven (popularity and credibility are assumed), making him a potentially good match for the brand or product.

Trying to assimilate and align all of these different indices and methodologies can be mind numbing. A company should start by identifying celebrities in which it is interested, then ascertain the popularity (and thus their attractiveness) of each by using the various indexes, the Q Score, DBI and Nielsen ratings. Once they have narrowed the pool of potential celebrities, the company needs to determine subjectively if the celebrity's image aligns with its brand or product. A mismatch here can lead to disastrous results, such as when Bob Dylan, known for his political activism, appeared in a Victoria's Secret commercial serenading scantily clad models – it just did not fit. Once alignment is rationalized, it is important to evaluate the trustworthiness and credibility of the celebrity in the context of promoting the particular product or brand by asking whether the celebrity's endorsement of this brand is credible. Here, the company can use using either the T.E.A.R.S., No TEARS, or 14-Point method. In the example of Dylan's endorsement of Victoria's Secret lingerie, the answer should have been a resounding "no." Using many of the points of analysis identified

114

above, the company can be fairly confident when choosing the celebrity to endorse its product or brand. The successful campaigns hit a "perfect storm" of these elements, aligning the product with the celebrity at the exact peak of that celebrity's career, such as when Kellogg's aligned a nutritionally wholesome breakfast cereal with a Heisman Trophy winning quarterback, Doug Flutie in the highly profitable "Flutie Flakes" campaign.

This brings up the final step in measuring a celebrity endorsement campaign: quantifying its success on a financial basis. This last measure requires constant monitoring of the costs of all components, modes, media, outlets, and demographics during the course of the campaign in order to evaluate whether the campaign is producing the desired result, whether that be brand awareness or increased sales. If the impact on the goal is minimal, the company will want to eliminate that particular partnership and move on to another. If the campaign is producing positive results, the company will want to retain that celebrity and further enhance its marketing using the celebrity. This kind of progression can be seen in the work of Dennis Haysbert for Allstate. What started as primarily voice over work ended up being a partnership wherein Haysbert took on a greater role as their official spokesperson and appears in every Allstate commercial, which end with his voice saying either "Are you in good hands" or "That's Allstate's stand." Haysbert's silky deep voice and solid personality is now practically synonymous with the "good hands" of Allstate.

Finally, after a series of continued successes, the best course for the company may be to partner with the celebrity in order to grow a niche business, much like Nike did with Michael Jordan, at first using him for endorsements, but eventually growing him into a unique brand. Utilizing this type of trajectory, a company can achieve that hallowed state of singularity between their endorser and their product.

Elements of Licensing

Although credit is often given to Shirley Temple as the first to exploit her celebrity persona through licensing a line of look-alike dolls, the real progenitor of the licensing industry in the United States is Charles C. "Cash & Carry" Pyle, a theatrical promoter and showman turned sports agent. In the mid 20's, Pyle recognized the connection between showmanship and sports celebrities. His first client was He the most renowned football star of the day, Harold "Red" Grange, a/k/a the "Galloping Ghost" who he signed in 1925 and negotiated perhaps the first multi-year contract for a football player, earning Grange $3,000 per game. He started the first American Football League which competed with the NFL.

One year later Pyle entered into an agency agreement with the French tennis legend and Wimbledon champion, Suzanne Lenglen, for the rumored sum of $50,000. To showcase Lenglen, he established the very first professional tennis tour through the U.S. and Canada featuring Lenglen playing legendary U.S. tennis player Mary K. Browne.

Pyle shrewdly exploited his celebrity athletes by soliciting and negotiating various licensing deals for movies, books, merchandise, and product endorsements which netted him and his clients hundreds of thousands of dollars in an age that was much less celebrity obsessed than we are today.

"C.C. Pyle," as he was also known, teaches us several valuable lessons about exploiting celebrity. First, he employed what we now call "guerilla marketing" by creating a revenue stream where none had previously existed. In both instances, Pyle established and promoted circuit tours, *i.e.*, games and matches in various cities nationwide, selling tickets to the events to showcase the talents and skills of his clients. These types of tours or "seasons" are something we now take for granted a part of professional sports. Secondly, Pyle realized that his marketing efforts would increase the popularity of these star athletes so he figured out a way to "cross sell" other things to their loyal fans, licensing their popularity in other types of media to product product to be sold on tour.

Pyle made it look easy. There is an old adage that everyone hears when they first start investing in the stock market: "buy low, sell high!" Simple enough right? Wrong. Anyone who has spent any time buying and selling shares of stock knows that there are many factors that complicate what seems like common sense. The same can be said for the exploitation of intellectual property. Anyone can create a copyright, a trademark or even come up with an innovation that is entitled to patent protection.

Likewise, every person has a right of publicity, either in common law or statute or, as we've seen, perhaps both. But once you've acquired your intellectual property, the saying goes, it's not worth anything until someone is willing to pay you something for it. The new proposal for copyright reform prepared by the Copyright Office in early 2015 recommends using this type of "willing seller, willing buyer" model. Unfortunately, that's the same kind of empty logic as the "buy low, sell high" method of stock purchasing. Of course you buy at the lowest price you can, that goes without saying. But that does not consider historical performance, profit/loss ratios, valuation, and market factors affecting the ebb and flow of stock prices. It also goes without saying that intellectual property has no value until it someone pays you for it. Like stock investing, exploitation of intellectual property is also filled with complexities and intricacies, and it is not always as simple as finding a "willing buyer" just because you're a "willing seller."

While the right of publicity gives a person the exclusive control over what happens commercially with their name, likeness and other attributes, that person will likely *not* find a willing buyer until that person somehow becomes a celebrity or does something that creates *value* in that persona. There is an old expression in Nashville that "it all begins with a song." The same can be said here about celebrity endorsement. It all begins with a "star." But like a good song, a persona does not have value until there is someone who desires to give you money for it.

Assuming that a person has found someone who is willing to pay compensation for their rights of publicity, what is the appropriate way to convey that right to them? In legal terms, this is called a license, which is a legal document that gives someone permission to do (or not to do) something. In terms that most everyone can relate to, think about the driver's license a state issues granting you permission to drive a vehicle on state roads. Or, consider a marriage license that gives two people permission to get married. Each of those are simple forms of "social contracts" between the state and individual citizens granting them permission to do something.

The legal realm of licensing is very similar, except that they are characterized as "private contracts." These private licenses show up in all areas of entertainment. For example, if you're a songwriter entering into an exclusive songwriting agreement with a publisher, you generally grant that publisher the copyrights to your songs. If you are an attractive actor starring in a feature film, you might enter into a nudity rider granting the producer the right to film parts of your naked body. Recording artists and other celebrities often grant third parties a license to use their name and likeness in promoting the goods that are created as a result of the partnership, whether they be recordings or films. A location release is a type of license granting someone permission to create an audiovisual work on the premises of a notable building or location and then further exploit that creation. And, of course, a celebrity's endorsement is granting the company permission to use that celebrity's likeness, name, and other attributes in association with its product or brand. All of these types of contracts are licenses that grant some type of permission.

Licensing is the most effective way of creating value in intellectual property. In 2012, "The Licensing Letter" reported that the global market for sales of licensed merchandise was in excess of $158 billion dollars. This industry involves the use of trademark, copyright, rights of publicity, logos, slogans, images, and other forms of intellectual property in many sectors spanning across fashion, novelty, and collegiate items to art, character, music, and sports. And let's not forget celebrity licensing. The licensing industry challenges the rights holders to think outside the box and be creative. Once an initial market is created, it is important to recognize the opportunity and expand the market by broadening the celebrity's reach in other media and outlets.

Some might wonder whether exploiting a license holds any real value. Would it not be better to hold the exclusive right to something and keep it to yourself rather than allowing others to exploit it? While that might be true in certain circumstances, there are many advantages to licensing intellectual property. First, licensing allows an entity to expand its reach into new markets without the need to fund manufacturing costs. Second, through licensing, an entity can generate new sources of revenue based on the brand's loyalty, reputation, and goodwill. Third, licensing allows an entity to expand its geographic reach without the need for relocation. Finally, a good licensing strategy will increase profit margins because there is no capital investment. This cost-shifting strategies works well not only for trademarks and goodwill, but for celebrity exploitation as well.

Take McIlhenny Company, for example, which started live as a business way down on Avery Island, Louisiana. The remote company became famous for selling Tabasco brand hot  sauce. As they sell more and more hot sauce, scaling the operation to meet demand for the brand can become expensive. Scaling a business to meet increased demand is always a great challenge for entrepreneurs and start up ventures. Not only does the company have to expend increasingly large sums of money to fulfill orders, but they have to increase in order to anticipate the demand.

What is the solution to scaling? If the company licenses its intellectual property to other manufacturers across the country, it will be able to outsource the manufacturing without the cost of building multiple factories or fulfilling orders. This is how McIlhenny expanded the geographic reach of its product without moving from its remote locality or spending precious capital.

Once a company scales its production sufficiently to meet demand, it can consider cross-licensing its intellectual property. If demand for the hot sauce is high enough to create scaling issues, the loyal consumers will likely enjoy the taste of hot sauce in other types of food products, such as BBQ sauce or potato chips. If consumers are that loyal to the brand, they might also like to "spice" up their wardrobe with various articles of clothing featuring the Tabasco logo, or purchase trinkets or other items for their home featuring the brand. The possibilities are endless.

All of the usages of the trademark and brand of McIlhenny generate new sources of revenues for the company without the need for any financial outlay. The only requirement is that they grant these other parties' permission to use their intellectual properties – trademarks, copyrights and patents - for specific and defined purposes. As a result of its licensing strategy, the Tabasco brand is recognized in over 150 countries worldwide and McIlhenny has generated revenues in excess of 250 million per year of which over 25% is pure profit margin.

No discussion of licensing would be complete without discussing the king of the industry in the realm of entertainment, The Walt Disney Company. Disney has always been a worldwide leader in global licensing, at times garnering as much as a 24% share worldwide. The first thing people generally think about when they think Disney is, of course, their famous theme parks in Florida and California, but the company is so much more of a conglomerate than that. Its portfolio of intellectual property is astounding. In addition to the obvious recreation sector, Disney has literally hundreds of subsidiaries and affiliated companies in areas such as film production and distribution, broadcasting, radio, television stations and networks, theater, books, magazines, music, sports, and the Internet. Each of those subsidiaries holds a portfolio of diversified brands and intellectual properties.

Each of Disney's properties are instantly recognizable to most consumers. In the television market, Disney owns ABC, ESPN, A&E, Lifetime, The History Channel, E!, and others, as well as Comcast, MedioOne, and Liberty Media, as well as production companies like Buena Vista and Touchstone. In film production and distribution, Disney owns LucasFilms, Marvel Entertainment, Touchstone, Pixar, Miramax, Hollywood and others. Their publishing holdings include Hyperion, US Weekly, ESPN Magazine, and the St. Louis Daily Record. Disney owns the Mighty Ducks and Angels sports franchises in Anaheim. It also has a very close partnership with The Hearst Corporation, which owns additional television stations and newspapers. Finally, of course, Disney owns a plethora of characters and content, such as Mickey Mouse and Winnie the Pooh and his gang, as wells as the Cars franchise, the Muppets, and other classic children's icons, and Disney Consumer Product to exploit those characters. The sheer breadth of their reach in the entertainment industry is mind-boggling.

All of these holdings garnered Disney a revenue of over $39 billion in 2013, giving them the top spot in most rankings of licensing entities. But the more informative insight that Disney provides is the cross-licensing that the company can do with all of its holdings. By owning film distribution subsidiaries, an animated film produced by Pixar will have an instant outlet through LucasFilms and can, perhaps, feature one of Disney's myriad characters, such as Winnie the Pooh, Mickey Mouse, or even one of the many Marvel characters. The soundtrack to the movie will feature songs owned and recorded by Lyric Street Records. The film can receive instant reviews in any of Disney's newspapers or magazines and have instant advertising on its television channels and radio broadcast. Finally, when the movie comes out, Disney Consumer Products will license the intellectual property to be produced as toys. All of this licensing activity is designed to work in harmonious unison to exploit the content, brand, and intellectual property of Disney. If *Dancing with the Stars* needs music to perform in connection with the dances, it can go to Buena Vista Music, Five Hundred South Songs, or one of its many other music publishing holdings. Cross-licensing ingenuity has made Disney the savant of licensing and has served as a model for many other conglomerates. For our purposes, it can serve as inspiration for a celebrity that wants to build a portfolio of intellectual property in industries that are not related to their professions or skills and use their celebrity to exploit them through the myriad avenues of licensing.

Licensing opportunities are available for any type of celebrity, be they movie actors, musicians, television stars or athletes. As mentioned at the start of this chapter, in 1934 Shirley Temple licensed her persona to the Ideal Novelty and Toy

Company for the purpose of manufacturing composition dolls. She was one of the first celebrities to do so, and she profited greatly, as the dolls generated over $45 million in revenues before 1941. For that period, an astounding feat. Sophia Lauren, the popular Italian movie star and legend, led the way in fragrance licensing with the release of her *Sophia* perfume in 1980. Now, almost any movie starlet worth her weight has a fragrance.

Another successful licensing venture was guitarist Les Paul's licensing deal with Gibson Guitar Corporation in the early 50's, one of the first licensing deals to be struck by a musician. The company has sold so many of its "Les Paul" guitars that in a

trademark infringement action in Finland, one court ruled that the name had become a common noun for guitars of a certain type and, therefore, was a generic name not entitled to trademark protection. But the title of the most prolific licensing musicians has to go to the rock band KISS who, beginning in 1977, has licensed over 5,000 products, outselling merchandise by the Beatles and Elvis combined.

Television celebrities are prime candidates for licensing. Beginning in 1976, Aaron Spelling produced the wildly popular television show *Charlie's Angels*, which churned out a wealth of licensing opportunities for him and his stable of actresses as well, Farrah Fawcett, Jaclyn Smith, Kate Jackson and, later, Cheryl Ladd and others. Most young boys in those days had one or more Farrah Fawcett posters hanging on their wall. Like Jennifer Aniston in the 90's, Fawcett was so popular that her hairstyle created a trend, both becoming synonymous with types of haircuts known as the "Farrah" or the "Aniston." Smith

successfully parlayed her celebrity into a lucrative fashion line that is still sold through K-Mart more than 40 years later.

While we're on the topic of licensing opportunities for television celebrities, let us not forget Jerry Seinfeld, whose popular nightclub act turned sitcom is one of the most syndicated programs (read, "licensed") of all time and is still going strong, with reruns playing nightly on cable television around the world.

The Seinfeld enterprise continues to churn out licensing deals, with almost every memorable phrase from the series plastered on either a t-shirt, hat, baseball cap, or mug (among many other tchotchkes): These pretzels are making me thirty; Festivus for the rest of us; Vandelay Industries; Serenity Now; and, of course "Hello Newman." These examples illustrate that licensing persona can build longevity in a celebrity's career, not matter what their art, and serve as a sustained stream of revenue long after the celebrity's star has lost its brightness, and even after it has expired, as it were.

We began this chapter discussing several sports figures who the earliest to take advantage of licensing opportunities. The trend continues as there are many modern sports celebs who find ways to exploit their fame. Andre Agassi endorsed and promoted the "Rebel" camera as a spinoff of his early radical personality. Evaonne Goolagong won over 14 tennis titles, but when she retired she launched her own line of active wear sold through Sears Roebuck & Co. Venus Williams followed suit with her own line of clothing, as do many of the great tennis stars. And, of course, who can forget Joe Namath's multiple endorsement opportunities during his heyday for Brut Cologne, Hanes panty hose, and other products.

But lest you think that it necessarily takes being at the forefront of your career as some sort of celebrity to be successful in licensing, our modern society provides evidence that almost anyone can gain fame for any reason and spin it off into a licensing opportunity. America was first exposed to the Kardashians on reality television, but they built their fame into a multi-million-dollar licensing conglomerate. Paris Hilton, of the Hilton hotel family fame, was one of the first "sex tape" celebrities. She launched a chain of celebrity-branded stores that has over 45 locations and is part of Hilton's $1.5 billion international empire. The power of licensing is that it can create celebrity where originally there was none.

There is no doubt that licensing is one of the leading generators of income for celebrities. In the past, major celebrities looked on those who appeared in advertisements as betraying their craft, not being a "true" artist, or as a celebrity that couldn't find work. Some celebrities, such as Tom Cruise, still have that antiquated opinion of endorsements and you will likely never see him in any type of licensing situation. But in today's media-driven world, that taboo is gone and should be forgotten. Now, well-bred actors take advantage of the incredible opportunities provided by licensing. Matthew McConaughey appeared in "scene" commercials for Buick. Academy award actors James Earl Jones and Gene Hackman do multiple voiceovers. No longer is exploitation of one's personality anathema.

As a representative handling the licensing for these celebrities, it is important to understand how and what to license. One of the most basic elements to look for in a license is the *grant*, after all, remember that a license grants someone permission. In regard to the celebrity, the grant will usually be for one of the following three intellectual properties, regardless of whether they are living or dead: copyright, trademark, and/or right of publicity. The first steps in examining any deal is to identify which of these broad rights are involved, prepare an "inventory" of sorts, and then determine what elements of that inventory are being used. A license should very clearly define what intellectual property rights are being granted to the licensee. For example, if a photograph of a celebrity is being used in an advertisement, the copyright in the photograph will need to be licensed, as will the right of publicity of the celebrity. You will also need to clear the rights in the photograph, in other words, make sure that the photograph does not claim a right in the photograph or that he has transferred the right to your celebrity. Or, if an advertising agency wants to hire an actor to be the "voice" of a particular brand, *only* the voice will be licensed. This is an oversimplified summary of a process that in legal circles is called "clearance."

The process of clearance involves obtaining any rights that are implicated by the proposed license. Using a musical composition in a television sitcom requires clearing that use with the songwriter and music publisher. If you are using a sound recording of that song, you will also need to obtain a license from the record label. Book publishers traditionally expend a great deal of resources clearing the use of quotes, resources, artwork, and photographs for their publications. Shooting a film generally requires a team of lawyers to work through the various licenses needed for location, actors, music, script, and other elements of the final product, as well as the licensing for the distribution of the film.

Another important principle in licensing that often gets implicated during the clearance stage is that in order to grant a license, the licensor must have the *authority* to grant the license, either through creation, ownership, license. or some type of assignment, and the intellectual property being licensed *must be protected by law.* For example, in the case of photographs of dead actors, it will be necessary to determine who has the authority to grant a license to use the image. It might be owned by the studio for whom the actor worked, the photographer who created the work, or the heirs of the actor. Earlier, we examined the case involving this issue with regard to the famous "steam grate" photograph of Marilyn Monroe.

As to the legal protectability, several of the cases reviewed point to the fact that, especially in regard to dead celebrities, there is often uncertainty as to whether the licensor has the right to license the intended property. In the cases of Marilyn Monroe and Jimi Hendrix, several courts have, indeed, determined that the law does not protect those rights and, therefore, the licensor does not have the right to grant the license.

The next stage is to clearly define the *scope* of the license, including a clear description of what is being licensed, what campaign it will be used for, and/or what product is being produced. In this phase, it is very important to identify whether the license will be exclusive or non-exclusive. In other words, if the celebrity is licensing use of her name for a perfume to be produced by Revlon, may she solicit other manufacturers to produce different fragrances and/or advertise for them, or is Revlon the only manufacturer who can produce perfume during the term. An exclusive deal should drive up the royalty percentage and any related advances.

If a celebrity's persona is being licensed for production of a product, additional considerations will be required as to the specifics and quality of the end product. If Franklin Mint is producing a figurine of an athlete to sell in its "Famous Quarterback" collection, for argument sake, the celebrity's representative will want to identify the product with specificity, *i.e.*, "a 1/16 scale molded ceramic figurine." In order to assure that they are manufactured to the highest quality standards necessary, the celebrity may require the manufacturer to submit artwork and depictions of the product and, finally, submit a sample model of the end product for evaluation. Finally, the celebrity will want to know the quantity of the initial production run, how many the company thinks it will sell, and how the company intends to market the product.

If those factors are the "what" and "why" of the licensing, a couple of other important questions are always "when" and "where." In legal terms, we call that the "term" and the "territory" of the licensing agreement, and they are not always as straightforward as they seem. The territory of an agreement refers not only to the geographic area in which the intellectual property may be exploited, *e.g.*, "the United States and its contiguous territories and possessions," but also to potential market or, more appropriately, the "distribution channel." A license deal can be limited, for example, to direct to consumer outlets such as QVC and the Home Shopping Network, and only in the U.S. It can always be very broad, encompassing the retail and wholesale channels throughout the world.

As for the length of the deal, referred to as the term, that can be stated in a simple number of years or it can be set up in the form of one initial term, with options than can exercised at either the discretion of the licensor or the licensee for different purposes. The option can also be contingent on certain requirements, such a minimum quantity of sales within the period or payment of a guaranteed royalty. To continue with the earlier illustration, if Peyton Manning is the celebrity negotiating with the Franklin Mint for production of ceramic figures, he would be able to negotiate a favorable guaranteed payments and/or minimum royalties for the first year of the term, and if those minimum royalty guarantees is not met, or the guaranteed payments are not paid, then Franklin Mint would not be given the opportunity to exercise the option and "renew" the contract. A guaranteed payment differs from a guaranteed royalty in a subtle way: the guaranteed payment is a flat sum that is decided in advance and must be paid in accordance with a defined schedule regardless of the royalties generated, while the guaranteed minimum royalty is based on calculation of a certain level of sales. If the defined level of sales is not obtained, the licensor may only receive the minimum royalty or perhaps may only be able to terminate the license. If the licensee is able to make the guaranteed payments, or meet the guaranteed minimum royalty, the option reverts back to the licensee and they have the right to renew the contract and continue selling or terminate the contract if sales are not as good as they had hoped.

Once the term ends and the contract expires either according to its own provisions or by termination, another consideration that is often neglected is what happens to the inventory. The licensing company will not want to be stuck with existing product that it has to store in its warehouse or inventory that has been distributed to wholesalers or is otherwise in the stream of commerce. The parties should agree on definitive terms for a "sell-off" period allowing costly inventory to be disposed of or returned to the licensor.

Then comes the fun part: counting the money or, as the title of this book suggests, "counting stars." The real reason most celebrities want to do this type of licensing deal is for the additional revenue streams which, in this structure, are called "royalties." As with any type of deal, the compensation is always negotiable. A royalty can be structured many ways. The easiest way to structure a royalty, and perhaps the most advantageous for the licensee, i.e., the one using the intellectual property, is a flat annual fee, without any upside. For the celebrity, any type of flat fee should be negotiated as advances and/or guarantees, so that everyone knows exactly what is to be paid. Most deals, however, are structured as percentage deals based on either net or gross sales. This is where guaranteed royalty structures can be beneficial for the celebrity. Obviously, the most beneficial type of percentage deal for the celebrity would be one that is based on a percentage of gross sales. If the discussion turns to net sales, it almost always benefits the manufacturer or licensee and great care should be exercised to determine exactly what can be deducted from gross.

If you are analyzing a net deal, the critical component will be the definition of "net." Obviously, the more deductions that are allowed, the less the licensor, or in our case the celebrity, receives. First, do not assume that the calculation starts with the gross figure. Some agreements allow deductions from gross *before* the calculations begin. Record labels in the 90's were notorious for charging what they called "container fees," and as such often provided that their net sales were based on "90% of gross sales" to allow for the costs of containers. Some deals calculate on the basis of wholesale sales, or the price at which the distributor sells the product to the retailer. It is generally acceptable for net sales to include deductions for shipping freight, taxes, credits, returns, and discounts made at time of sale. Credits and returns, however, should be limited to "bona fide" returns or those credits "actually paid." Less desirable are deductions for common business expenses such as sales commissions, debts, uncollectible accounts, promotions, marketing, and advertising. Any time the word "fee" appears in a licensing agreement, it is a red flag and should be questioned. One means by which a celebrity can assure that he or she is being paid the appropriate amount is to assure that the accounting provisions to require licensee to provide its "source" documents, *i.e.*, the billing invoice submitted to and paid by the wholesaler or retailer, in order to ascertain exactly how much the party received for the product.

In today's post Wal-Mart world, if you are negotiating a license for the manufacturing of a product, it is likely being produced oversees, probably in China. For this reason, in these types of deals, you may see the term "landed costs." The landed cost of a product refers to the total cost of a shipment of goods, including purchase price, freight, insurance, and other costs up to the port of destination. In some instances, it may also include the customs, duties and other taxes levied on the shipment. This is then used to determine a "per piece" price on which you can base various royalty structures.

Several nuances can come in to play when you are negotiating licenses for specific members of a large unit. If you represent a driver for a NASCAR automobile does that driver, for instance, have the right to negotiate a deal with Mattel to produce a Hot Wheels replica of the vehicle, or do you need to clear that through NASCAR? This relates back to the concept of having the proper authority to grant the rights being licensed. The same principle applies to players for any major league such as the NFL, NBA, NHL, and MLB, among others. You should not assume that the person you represent has all the rights needed in order to grant someone the permission necessary to do what they want to do. These major conglomerates also frequently enter into their own endorsement deals for certain products, to the exclusion of the individual teams within their organization. For example, during the most recent NFL season, Motorola was replaced by Bose as the "official" NFL headphone. As part of that deal, several NFL players who had exclusive endorsement deals with Beats headphones could no longer wear that brand of headphones on the field or in connection with NFL sanctioned activities, since they had provisions in their agreements with their franchise to observe the licensing requirements of the parent ship.

Finally, for celebrities with large social networks and fan bases should attempt to position themselves as joint venture partners with the licensing entity in order to achieve maximum revenues. The pioneers of licensing discussed in the early part of the chapter laid the groundwork for future generations, and as a result, most celebrities today, and perhaps even more so their teams, recognize the value and power of brand and lifestyle licensing as an invaluable marketing tool and an essential corollary to their careers. The licensing principles discussed in this chapter can help propel the celebrity from the clicking shutters of the red carpet to the massive exposure and wealth that a powerfully crafted brand can create.

Branding & Endorsement Trends, Concepts, & Strategies

As we've seen, throughout the centuries, people who have achieved a certain level of fame and notoriety have allowed others to build on that fame and add credibility to their brand or product through the concept of licensing, giving them permission to market products using their name and persona. To summarize, licensing is an essential component in transforming a successful sports figure, comedian, actor, musician, expert talent, or otherwise celebrity into a global brand and cultural icon. Strategic branding through effective licensing has the ability to provide "mailbox money," *i.e.*, ongoing annuity revenues for the long term, even into retirement and for future generations. That is the kind of money that you can lie in bed at night and know you're still earning.

This is a good strategy for sports figures whose bodies quickly fail under the intense physical pressure and actors and actresses whose beauty will eventually fade. Good licensing and endorsement strategies can also increase a celebrity's Q and DBI scores, keeping the celebrity's image in the forefront of people's mind and increasing their cultural influence well past the height of their careers. The creation of a licensed and branded product line enables a celebrity to extend his or her net worth beyond their limited entertainment careers by offering consumers authentic products to experience in their everyday lives, products which remind them of how much they loved the celebrity in the first place.

To accomplish this goal of longevity, it important for the celebrity to surround themselves with professionals who can work with them to achieve their long-term goals. A good agent or manager can find a celebrity multiple opportunities that would not be available to them otherwise. A good entertainment attorney can assist the manager or agent in drafting and closing the licensing deals. A good accountant and/or financial advisor will not only help the celebrity vet the financial viability of potential deals, but can also help the celebrity plan for retirement and for leaving something behind for heirs. This team of professionals can help the astute celebrity plan a strategy that will insure creation of longevity.

While brand and product endorsements are lucrative for celebrities, these types of opportunities may become scarcer as the celebrity's star reaches its zenith and begins to fade. No doubt, a celebrity has to exploit every good opportunity during the momentum, riding the waves and capitalizing on their fame while they are "hot." But the smart celebrity will go beyond these "one off" deals and create opportunities that have a long term potential, perhaps being an active partner in the licensing deals or a shareholder in the corporation, or becoming entrepreneurs in a particular industry, or even becoming a venture capitalist, investing in ventures of which he or she is a part.

Ryan Seacrest, the well-known, hardworking radio show host, host of *American Idol*, and replacement host for Dick Clark's *Rockin' New Year's Eve*, is a good illustration of a celebrity that has capitalized on the momentum of his fame. Seacrest became an entrepreneur in an area he knows a lot about, television production, when he formed Ryan Seacrest Production. By doing so, he wisely exploited his brand loyalty and expanded it at the same time. The production company produces programming for several networks, including E! and MTV. Seacrest upped the ante when he teamed up with the largest U.S. radio company, Clear Channel, who committed $300 million to partner with Ryan in the production company. But the icing on the cake, and the component that really sets him up for life, is that Seacrest also teamed up with the equity firms that fund Clear Channel, Thomas H. Lee Partners and Bain Capital, to identify new investments and acquisitions.

The prime example of another celebrity turned venture capitalist is Ashton Kutcher, who started his career as a model, but then later landed a role on the Fox sitcom, *That '70s Show* and, still later, took Charlie Sheen's place on *Two and Half Men*. Kutcher proved to be a shrew businessman, negotiating a "position" as a product engineer for Lenovo, a company he also endorsed in several television commercials. He was part of the VOIP service, Ooma where he served as Creative Director, spearheading marketing and producing viral videos to promote the company. Kutcher, together with his manager Guy Oseary and billionaire investor Ron Burkle, formed a company called A-Grade Investments. A-Grade is a venture capital firm that specializes in seed money and series A round investments. Most notably, A-Grade invested in Spotify, Uber, Shazam, Soundcloud, and Airbnb. Aston also owns interests in several restaurants in New York, L.A. and Atlanta. A major lesson we can draw from Kutcher is his incorporation of a new trend in the arena of celebrity endorsements wherein the celebrity becomes part of the management team and/or an "employee" in charge of some component of the company such as marketing. This is not to take away from Kutcher – he is an active participant in managing the companies he endorses – but it guides the new celebrity toward a very lucrative strategy. Rather than just being the face or voice of a company, be an active participant and even own a piece.

Nick Adler is a branding agent at the marketing agency, Cashmere, representing Snoop Dogg. Snoop Dogg, somewhat like Kutcher, has attained the status of "venture capitalist" investing in over fifteen companies such as Ustream, Reddit, and others. Snoop Dogg has grown from being known as a recreational drug user and hip hop singer to a successful business man, wearing sweater vests and hanging out in Palo Alto with people like Larry Page of Google. "[A]t the end of the day is the relationships," said Adler. Although Adler says that he and Snoop Dogg "didn't have a dedicated strategy" he indicates that Snoop Dogg is methodically quiet when he considers an investment pitch, taking it all in until he gets it, and then he "opens up" to speak and "just owns the room."[55] Methodical plotters like Snoop Dogg will be reaping the rewards of endorsement partnerships for years to come. The lesson that Snoop Dogg teaches us is the importance of a trusted business partner to guide your exploitations.

Other celebrities who have been bitten by the VC bug include actor Will Smith, singer Justin Timberlake, rappers Jay-Z, Curtis Jackson (50 Cent), and athletes Steve Young and Rob Dyrdek, just to name a few. This VC trend includes actors, singers, rappers, comedians, athletes, talent managers, and fashion moguls investing in a broad range of industry sectors including the Internet, mobile technology, telecommunications, consumer products, consumer services, restaurants, food & beverage, traditional media, healthcare, leisure, and software. This nascent trend of celebrity investors has also caught the eyes of the entertainment industry, where bulwark companies such as Creative Artist Agency, one of the top entertainment agencies in the country, is rumored to be developing a $20 million venture fund.

Another important strategy to consider is the so-called "exit strategy." Just as critical as knowing which deals to invest in is the determination of when to cash in. Jackson/50 Cent acquired a minority shareholder in Energy Brands (Vitamin

---

[55] Greenfield, Rebecca. Snoop Dogg, Investor: How the Famed Rapper claimed his Spot among Serious Celebrity VC's. Fast Company. October 31, 2014.

Water/Glaceau) as a part of his endorsement of the product, which was ultimately sold to Coca-Cola for $4.1 billion. Jay-Z formed a footwear company Rocawear in 1999 with his A-Fella Records co-founder Damon Dash, using celebrity endorsements to propel the company to annual sales in the neighborhood of $700 million. They sold the company to Iconix Brand Group in 2007 for over $200 million dollars. Finally, Dr. Dre and producer Jimmy Iovine sold their incredibly success headphone company, Beats, along with the streaming music service of the same name, to Apple for $3.2 billion in perhaps one of the most over-inflated valuations in recent history, making Dr. Dre one of Forbe's top ten riches celebrities at an estimated net worth of around $800 million. Sometimes, the present day value of that kind of capital is worth much more than the headaches of running the business. Good investors are always looking for the best exit strategy.

Most of these examples involve celebrities and/or companies who are already at the top of their respective industries entering into a mutually beneficial deal. But what if you are on the outside looking in, someone who is trying hard to become the "celebrity" that everyone wants to be. Sometimes "making it" requires guerilla tactics to coax a celebrity to endorse a product, as in the example of my longtime client, Daymond John, and his rise to the top of the fashion and branding industry through the creation of FuBu. He started that company with an idea he got from seeing a rap group wearing an unusual "tie-top" hat, which was not widely available. With about forty dollars' worth of material, and sewing instructions from his mother, John created a few dozen hats and sold them on a street corner in Queens, New York, garnering a profit of $800. "I knew I was on to something," Daymond reminisced. But John's big break came when his relentless pursuit of local rising rap star LL Cool J finally convinced the rapper to pose for a photograph wearing one of John's FUBU shirts. "I wouldn't be where I am if people in the neighborhood hadn't helped me out," he told John when he finally acquiesced to the photograph.

John scrapped some money together and took the photograph to a major trade show in Las Vegas, landing $400,000 in orders. But the story doesn't end there. On the flight back from Las Vegas to New York, John began to sweat trying to figure out to fill those lucrative orders! After being turned down by two dozen banks for loans, John and his mother decided to take a second mortgage on the house to fulfill the purchase orders.[56] The entrepreneurial efforts of Daymond and his mother continued when they decided to pay for a well-placed advertisement in the *New York Times* classified that attracted the attention of Samsung, known more for its textile production in Korea than for its more familiar electronics. Samsung struck a deal to invest in FuBu, and the rest is history.

This concept of giving celebrities and dignitaries product samples to grow a product developed into a recent trend of

---

[56] Lee, Ellen. "How FUBU Founder Daymond John Conquered Urban Fashion," CNBC, Small Business, August 7, 2002.

throwing parties and giving out "bling," or samples of the products, to the attendees in order to drive marketing, usually by encouraging the guests to "tweet" photos of themselves with the celebrities and their bling.

In fact, social media now plays a critical role in celebrity endorsement and is a technique that be applied by anyone. These days, most celebrities pay more attention to the number of followers, connections or friends they have on Twitter, Instagram, LinkedIN, and FaceBook that they do to Q Scores and other ratings indices. Almost any popular celebrity will have social network followers that number in the millions. You can rest assured that the higher this number is, the more a company seeking an endorsement from that celebrity will have to pay. It is a simple matter of supply and demand economics. If you want to connect your product (the supply) with a celebrity's demand (the followers), the price goes up. This issue is fast becoming one of the most negotiated sections of any celebrity endorsement deal with requirements for posting to social networks and sometimes the production of "viral videos" for posting to the celebrity's followers.

Street branding, endorsement acuity, and awareness of social media impact, is what made Daymond John the branding and licensing guru he is today. One of the unique services offered by John's New York-based company, Shark Branding, is creating and designing clothing and accessory lines for celebrities and assisting them with the implementation, distribution, and sale of clothing lines bearing their persona, and finally helping them navigate the world of fashion the way Daymond learned to do it on the streets. Sometimes you have to think outside the box. Now, celebrity clothing and accessory lines have exploded and anyone who has any reputation at all has a line of something, usually tied to a particular retailer. The Olsen sisters have a popular line of clothing at J.C. Penney; Miley Cyrus has her line at Wal-Mart; Selena Gomez has the "Dream Out Loud" line for K-Mart; and Madonna landed a line directed at "tweeners" distributed through Macy's. Well known actress of film and stage, Sarah Jessica Parker, used the technique mentioned earlier when Halston hired her to be President and CEO of a new fashion label for Halston, rumored to be worth around $10 million over the course of the deal. Whether it is fragrance, handbags, jewelry, accessories, hats, or apparel, fashion seems to be an area that is particularly suited for celebrity endorsements.

Early, mention was made of the many product placement techniques used in the sitcom *Seinfeld*. Product placements are very important tool in the licensing arsenal. These include items such as cereal boxes placed on the shelves of Jerry's apartment or story lines developed around the *Junior Mints* Kramer dropped in the open cavity of a surgery patient or the *JuJubes* candy Elaine stopped off to buy before visiting her hospitalized boyfriend. These examples highlight two types of product placement. The most basic is when a particular product is visible somewhere in a scene, but the character doesn't draw attention to it. These types

147

of placements generate smaller fees that help offset the cost of production. The more advance product placement is when a product is mentioned by name or even used by one of the characters or, as in the case of *Seinfeld*, where the product is actually integrated into the story line. These more advanced uses are types of "endorsements" and fetch a substantially higher fee.

These elements are no accident of course, and constitute a very old technique, now used by film makers and television producers to raise money for their productions, that developed as far back as the mid 1800's. It is rumored that then-popular novelist Jules Verne was solicited by several shipping and transport companies to appear in his upcoming novel *Around the World in Eight Days*, written in 1873. The book most certainly has references to prominent companies of the time, such as the East India Company, the Oriental Steamship Company, or the Peninsula Company, although there is no direct evidence to suggest that Verne was paid to include those references. Regardless, Verne taught the modern world an important lesson in product references: now prominent songwriters in L.A., New York, and Nashville can be paid large sums to mention a particular brand of truck or liquor in a musical composition, and popular authors most certainly take advantage of this technique. This process in not lost on Hollywood. It's no accident that many of the recent *Bond* films feature the latest BMW vehicles.

Payment for product placement really began to flourish more extensively with the advent of feature films. One early example is the collaboration between First National Pictures with the manufacturer of Corona typewriters for the appearance of their product in several of their films, including 1925's *The Lost World*. Even the Christmas classic *It's a Wonderful Life* features George Bailey with a copy of *National Geographic*, with aspirations of being a world explorer. Throughout the early days of television, the 1930's through the 1960's, many programs were underwritten by corporate sponsors. In fact, the phrase "soap operas" derives its name from that fact that they were often underwritten by manufacturers of consumer cleaning products, such as Procter & Gamble or Unilever, because it was anticipated that their primary audience would be housewives who, at the time, did most of the cleaning. Product placements or references can be used to acquire sponsorships by various creators, including actors, producers, songwriters, musicians, and sports figures.

One of the issues that often arise in the context of product placement is how the brand will be portrayed in the finished product. Often referred to as "product displacement," this is the idea that the advertisers do not want their product to appear in a non-flattering scene or context. For example, one of the primary sponsors of the film *Slumdog Millionaire* was Mercedes-Benz, whose executives were amenable to the cars being driven by gangsters, but did not want them featured in the scenes depicted in the slums.

Branding is nothing more than the culmination of all of the principles that we've been discussing. A brand can be a trademark, a celebrity or even a lifestyle. It can be all of those things rolled into one. The point is, once a celebrity has a significant market impact, the proper exploitation of that celebrity's right of publicity equates to a major branding effort using any or all of the techniques discussed in this chapter. The celebrity becomes the brand and it is up to his or her team to find new and creative ways to license that value.

Considerations for the Licensee

As noted earlier, contrary to an oft-quoted rumor, all publicity is *not* always good publicity, particularly in connection with a celebrity endorsement deal gone bad. Getting an endorsement from a celebrity does not necessarily guarantee a successful collaboration, and certainly does not guarantee increased sales for the product. For every successful campaign, there are a myriad of others that do not fare so well. From the perspective of the manufacturer or advertiser seeking the celebrity's endorsement, there are many considerations, in addition to the popularity and influence of the celebrity considered in earlier chapters, that must be taken into account in regard to an endorsement deal.

When considering a celebrity to lend his or her name, likeness, and endorsement to a new product line, for example, careful thought should go into what kind of brand equity that celebrity brings to the table and whether that fills a profitable void in the company's current lineup. Increasingly, licensees expect the celebrity to contribute in terms of designing the product and a commitment to marketing it. Sarah Jessica Parker's lucrative employment/endorsement deal with Halston is a prime example of colossal failure in this regard. The new line of clothing created by the partnership did not receive favorable reviews and, more importantly, tanked at the cash register, forcing Halston to bring in a liquidation company and pay Parker $3 million as exit money.

As the post Wal-mart era has shown us, retail space is expensive. Therefore, if a new product is going to succeed, it has to compete for floor space. Retailers are not going to eliminate the bestselling products in order to take a chance on something new. This is where celebrity endorsement can flourish. If the celebrity has the consumer cache to convince the retailer that the endorsed product has a shot at being successful, they can help the manufacturer convince the retailer to dedicate appropriate shelf space. The more prominent the celebrity is, the more a retailer is willing to take a chance. This is an extremely important consideration for a licensee when considering the amount of investment that is necessary to launch a new product.

In that context, the licensee also has to ask himself if his association with the celebrity will likely increase exposure and awareness of his product. This is where the metrics discussed earlier can prove beneficial. Perhaps a particular celebrity endorsement can help a company expand into a market where it did not have significant prior exposure. If a company is trying to market to an older audience, that need a celebrity whose DBI had Q Score is strong in that metric. The rise of the Baby Boomer generation is one good example of this, as consumer manufacturing companies and advertisers began to realize that the population was getting older. Pay close attention to television advertisements and you will notice the trend to use older, more established actors for products targeted to the aging population. Already, we are starting to see this influence on Hollywood, as they start to pump out more movies for older audiences.

As already noted in the previous chapter, the influence of the Internet and social media on endorsement deals is starting to play a major role. The concept of developing a "social media presence" is the byproduct of life on the Information Superhighway, as Al Gore called it. As a result, it is important for the celebrity and the marketer to work together to identify different ways to leverage the celebrity's social media contacts in creating a "buzz" about the new product. Many of my clients have been engaged to produce "viral videos" featuring the celebrity using the product. A well-known hip hop artist was paid handsomely to incorporate a scene in his latest music video featuring himself simply pouring a particular brand of liquor into an ice-filled glass, and then distribute that 15-second clip to his social media followers, which happen to number in the millions. It is important that the celebrity accentuate the unique features of the product or service so that it stands out, and to include the appropriate hashtags. As an aside, if you represent such a deal legally, you should make sure you accommodate for any applicable FDA regulations regarding advertisement of liquor. Loyal fan who sees their favorite celebrity "tweeting" a video of themselves using a product will drive the fans to the retail stores or Amazon to purchase it.

It is also important that both parties recognize the potential hurt feelings and bad publicity that can result from a deal gone bad or from a celebrity who has a "wardrobe malfunction" in the middle of s performance. When a photo of British supermodel Kate Moss in an allegedly cocaine-induced state of consciousness was splashed across the front page of the *Daily Mirror* and other tabloids worldwide, no less than half a dozen companies dropped Moss like a leper, including lucrative deals with Chanel and H&M. Bad publicity is not always good, and companies, particular those with certain standards to uphold, do not want their brand, product, and reputation tarnished by one foolish slip by a celebrity endorser. That is why most endorsement contracts or agreement involving celebrities involve what is sometimes referred to as "morals" clause which gives both parties an opportunity to terminate if either of them is engaged in an activity that would tend to bring harm to the reputation of the other. For this reason alone, many companies prefer the use of dead celebrities, who are not prone to publicity snafus, and cartoon characters as their spoke people, particularly conservative companies like insurance conglomerates, who lean more toward ducks and lizards. If celebrity endorsement campaigns are not carefully managed and reviewed periodically, they can quite literally ruin a brand or product overnight, think O.J. Simpson, convicted of murder, and its impact on his endorsement deal with Hertz. It can take a long time to rid a company's image of such negative stigmas.

The popularity and ubiquity of Nike, primarily as a result of its successful celebrity endorsement campaigns featuring Michael Jordon, led to the creation of another technique in branding and endorsements known as "lifestyle branding." Lifestyle branding using the concept of singularity to merge the image of the celebrity and the line of products into one, and then seeks to elevate the union as indicia of a lifestyle in the mind of a culture. Using many of the techniques discussed earlier in regard to the psychological underpinnings of celebrity endorsement, lifestyle brands are said to be a better way of allowing the consumer to express themselves and their identity by associating themselves with a symbol of a certain type of life. Lifestyle brands are intended to inspire, guide, and motivate the consumer, contributing to the definition of their way of life. A celebrity whose reputation or image is aligned with this type of lifestyle reinforces and supplements this philosophy. The companies that adopt an ideology will attract a relatively high number of people, thus potentially becoming a recognized social phenomenon.[57] It is easy to see why this technique has developed into such a commercial trend.

While certainly not the first at social branding, Apple certainly has marketed itself as a lifestyle. The biography of Steve Jobs provides insight into how they developed their company and

---

[57] Saviolo, Stefania; Marazza, Antonio, *Lifestyle Brands - A Guide to Aspirational Marketing*. Palgrave Macmillan (2012).

their brand based on three principles outlined by Apple marketing guru Mike Markkula who:

> wrote his principles in a one-page paper titled "The Apple Marketing Philosophy" that stressed three points. The first was *empathy*, an intimate connection with the feelings of the customer: "We will truly understand their needs better than any other company." The second was *focus*: "In order to do a good job of those things that we decide to do, we must eliminate all of the unimportant opportunities." The third and equally important principle, awkwardly named, was *impute*. It emphasized that people form an opinion about a company or product based on the signals that it conveys.[58]

The third trait is one that weaves itself into the lifestyle philosophy of branding by "imputing" its ideology into the minds of consumers. Apple has done an amazing job at defining itself as the preeminent design company with the unique perspective, focusing on core products that fulfill the specific needs of a specific type of consumer. As current CEO, Timothy D. Cook described it in one of Apple's now famous keynote speeches, "We believe in the simple, not the complex…. We believe that we're on the face of the Earth to make great products [and that means] saying no to thousands of projects so that we can really focus on the few that are truly important and meaningful to us."

Apple's corporate philosophy inspires a literal cult-like following of unquestioning automatons who defend the Apple products at all costs ("Apple-matons" if you will), sometimes in

---

[58] Isaacson, walter. *Steve Jobs.* Simon & Shuster, 2013.

the face of arguably better competition and other first movers, from whom they often borrow technology and ideas. But the fanatics are steadfastly loyal and almost worship the ground of its founder, Steve Jobs, and by proxy, its current CEO. In the eyes of its loyal fans, Apple can do no wrong, even to the point that they cannot tolerate negative portrayals of Steve Jobs such as the 2015 film biography of the same name. The fan culture they've built is very reminiscent of that of a celebrity.

But fashion moguls Calvin Klein and Abercrombie & Fitch are the more likely candidates to lay claim as the progenitors of this marketing approach of building a "culture" around their product. Thanks to their marketing styles, developed in the 1980's and 1990's, the country had its first glimpse at  what would later be referred to as "lifestyle branding." In 1981, Calvin Klein's launched an advertising campaign for "CK" jeans, featured Brooke Shields in the tight hip-hugging dungarees, provocatively unbuttoning her blouse, with her midriff showing in a somewhat suggestive pose. The television compliments to the print versions featured the provocative punch line "...want to know what comes between me and my Calvins?" Klein continued that campaign into the 90's, launching many celebrity careers, including those of Kate Moss and Mark Wahlberg who appeared in similar poses. The cultural phenomena that it inspired is reflected in one of the blockbuster movies of the time, *Back to the Future*, when Marty is transported back to the past in the time machine and his mother refers to him a "Calvin" because she sees the Calvin Klein waist band on his underwear. The latter is actually a combination of this technique with the technique of product placement discussed earlier.

Abercrombie & Finch also used the concept of lifestyle branding in the 1990's, although a bit more refined and subtle. Abercrombie, the retail mall clothing stores geared toward the teen market, grew its popularity by building its marketing campaign on the "retro" 1950's ideology of preppy, young Ivy League types, with advertisements featuring white, masculine beefcake shots that were reminiscent of that earlier era. The undertones of the campaign were in direct contrast to "political correctness," a prevailing trend at the time.

Many companies are founded on certain "lifestyles": Victoria's Secret evokes a rebellious contrast to the Victorian puritan attitude toward sex; Patagonia portrays itself as an environmentally friendly brand; Burberry intentionally conveys the hipster subculture of London; Gaiam conveys a natural, inner peace; and Nautica portrays the fresh, exhilarating feeling of being on a sailboat.

These examples serve to illustrate some of the key principles of a lifestyle brand. First, a lifestyle brand connects to the consumer on some basic need and conveys the impression that they are the only company that can deliver the stimulus needed to fulfill it. Apple, for example, successfully plants marketing seeds in all types of media when it releases a new product that literally inform the consumer that they are the only one. The company's latest offering at the time of this writing is a smart watch, something that has been around for over three years, manufactured by companies like Sony, LG, Motorola, and others. Yet in a review by its technology writer, Farhad Manjoo the *New York Times* says "the Apple Watch works like a first-generation device, with all the limitations and flaws you'd expect of brand-new technology." To the point, Apple's new product (at least at the time of this writing) is neither "first-generation" nor "brand-new technology," but the company successfully convinces or otherwise persuades writers for major news outlets to describe it as such, thereby convincing the consumer that Apple is the *only* company that can make a smart watch. In this way, the marketing infiltrates the *zeitgeist* and conveyed to people who repeat it in everyday conversation.

Secondly, the lifestyle brand stimulates the base need we all have to be part of a larger group, *i.e.*, to "fit in," and convinces the consumer that purchasing their brand creates an emotional connection to the group. This brings up back to the core philosophy underlying celebrity endorsements, the "leader of the pack" mentality. Apple's website copy for the new Apple Watch proclaimed:

> You won't just send and recieve messages, calls, and mail more easily and efficiently. You'll express yourself in new, fun, and more personal ways. With Apple Watch, every exchange is less about reading words on a screen and more about *making a genuine connection.*

Here, Apple doesn't mince any words but gets right to the point: by purchasing its version of the smart watch, you'll "express yourself" in "more personal ways" and make "a genuine connection." The underlying connotation is that all of the many smart watches that came before did not achieve this "genuine connection," rather only an Apple Watch can do that. To their adoring consumer, it does not matter that these statements are blatantly false marketing hype, the only thing that matters is that this product is the only one that will connect them to the "cult of Apple." Once the hype infiltrates the media, is passed down to the public, it is repeated to the faithful who become evangelists for the lifestyle.

Finally, the lifestyle brand embodies a disruptive philosophy and proposes an innovative viewpoint. These principles may be conveyed to the consumer in many ways. To continue with the example, Apple creates a serene and friendly shopping environment in its retail stores to emphasize the shopping experience. It employs "genius" staffers to provide individual services that presumably cannot be provide by more conventional service types. These are key factors to its lifestyle branding and they all harken back to the IBM of the 1970's with its blue shirted employees. Apple seeks to position itself as an iconoclastic company that establishes trends, regardless of the reality. Lifestyle brands tend to operate on the principle that *perception* is reality, which brings us full circle to Abraham Lincoln and the difference between the shadow and the tree. The tree doesn't matter so long as you can convince the public that they have to live in the shadow.

Whatever the perception a brand is trying to convey, finding a celebrity or an art form that serves as the embodiment of a corporate philosophy helps cement the lifestyle concept in the mind of the consumer and pull the image together into a cohesive message. The snowboarding company Burton did this by tapping into that subculture. When Apple began life with the Apple 1 in 1976, it focused on the markets that were neglected by the giant of the PC world in that era, IBM, giving discounts to schools, educational companies and nonprofits, and tapping into the arts and music subcultures. EA Sports tapped into a football icon, John Madden, to create Madden Football, a video game that has sold over 99 million copies over time and has propelled EA Sports into the premiere spot in its industry. Lifestyle branding is a culmination of the many techniques discussed in this chapter. A successful branding effort must incorporate all elements and philosophies of the company in order to successfully tap into the target culture and then analyze the metrics find cultural icons, *i.e.*, celebrities, to whom that market relates.

Frank Dileo & Final Thoughts

Talking about Michael Jackson...
It's not hard to become famous.
It's not hard to have a hit record,
But it's difficult to maintain your high level of career.
-Frank Dileo

If there is just one piece of advice I can give above all others when it comes to negotiating celebrity endorsements, it would be to think outside the box. I know that may sound a little cliché, but when it comes to the world of entertainment, what "has always been done that way" is too often the way things continue to get done, until someone comes along who is innovative and ballsy enough to say "we're not doing it that way." To become a "mover and shaker" in an industry as full of shock jocks and radical artists as the entertainment industry, you have to be an iconoclast. You have to insist, "we're doing it my way." To use a term that is perhaps overused in this arena, that's "disruptive" thinking. When I think about celebrities and endorsement deals in context of iconoclasts, there is one person that comes to my mind:

In the mid 2000's, I had the pleasure of meeting, and becoming good friends with, Frank Dileo, who managed the career of Michael Jackson on and off before their deaths in 2009 and 2011 respectively. Frank also managed the career of Cindi Lauper, launched the career of Boy George and REO, and was responsible for the success of many of the top-selling albums of the 70's and 80's. I've never met anyone as "disruptive" as Dileo. He was an iconoclast in every sense of that word, and most

certainly thought outside the box. When Frank entered a room, it was like a scene from a movie: everyone dropped what they were doing, the needle on the record player scratched as the music stopped playing abruptly, and the whole room stared at him. Frank Dileo was bigger than life, as the photograph from the cover of the *Nashville Scene* illustrates.

Frank began managing Jackson after the release of his quintessential breakout release of *Thriller* in 1984 and was instrumental in the production of the groundbreaking video for the title single. Frank cut his teeth in the music industry in the cutthroat business of independent record promotion, so he admittedly was no stranger to "payola." Although he never admitted it, Dileo always made references to organized crime syndicates and the mafia, though I could never be sure whether he was just pulling my leg. Frank was the perfect caricature of himself, always bucking the system while chewing or smoking a huge stogie, his hair slicked back, almost the living caricature of the roles he played in *GoodFellas* and *Wayne's World*.

One evening, he and I were sitting at a dimly-lit table in *Viragos*, a local Nashville nightclub, enjoying a few cocktails. When he drank, Frank waxed reminiscent. That night, he told me the story of negotiating the deal with Pepsi to employ Michael as a celebrity endorser. They were just on the heels of the *Thriller* video at the time, so Jackson was a valuable commodity. According to Frank, the *Thriller* album was responsible for saving the music industry:

> The Thriller album was selling an average of one million copies a week, which no other record in history had done. Michael Jackson, that year with the release of *Thriller*, saved the record business. Tower Records was going out of business. CBS itself had two black Fridays where they laid off like a thousand people. Many other record companies were going out of business, but *Thriller* was so big, it brought millions of people into the stores and hundreds of millions of dollars in profits.

So Frank knew he had the momentum going into the negotiation. Michael was riding the wave of one of the best-selling albums of all time and was on top of all of the charts, if not the whole world. In his heart, Frank knew that Pepsi really wanted Michael. It was a perfect match: Pepsi and Michael were both fighters. They were both symbols of a younger culture.

Up to that time, Pepsi consistently had lackluster sales compared to the market leader, Coca-Cola. As it so often does, it was trying to rebrand itself and capture a greater share of the youth market. To achieve this, Pepsi was working on a new campaign targeted at the "Next Generation." According to their marketing firm, "The goal was to make Pepsi look young and Coke look old."[59]

In November 1983, about a year after the *Thriller* album was released and the video became a success on MTV, both soda manufacturers were in hot pursuit of the fresh young talent. Negotiating with Frank for months, Coca-Cola struck first with a staggering, unheard-of offer to pay Jackson a cool $1 million. Before that offer, it was unusual to see six-figure compensation for celebrity endorsements of this type. But Frank told Michael that he wanted to see what Pepsi had to offer. Frank knew that Pepsi was a little more desperate than Coke and really needed Michael's influence with the youth of the country to pull off the new campaign. This is another important point, when you negotiate a deal of this magnitude, *do your homework*. Frank knew more about Pepsi and Coke than any person at that moment.

Armed with the unprecedented offer from Coke, Frank invited then-CEO of Pepsi, Roger Enrico, to fly with him from New York to California on a private Lear jet. Frank was no stranger to luxury in those days. While on the three to four-hour flight, Dileo challenged Enrico to consummate a better deal, informing him that such a move would propel Pepsi to market domination. As added incentive, he told Enrico that when he

[59] Herrera, Monica, "Michael Jackson, Pepsi Made Marketing History." Adweek. July 6, 2009.

landed in L.A., if he hadn't decided, he would to close the deal with his archrival and nemesis. Those last words must have cut Enrico deeply. When I pointed out to Frank that this was a "shotgun wedding" ultimatum which often backfires in negotiation, he reminded me that sometimes you do what you have to do to close the deal, particularly when you have the bigger hammer.

Dileo did not have to do too much convincing, of course, but he did remind Enrico that Michael was the "King of *Pop*," and certainly portrayed the face of that new generation Pepsi was trying to attract. Although I'm certain Frank did not use the word "singularity" or "celebrity/product alignment," he was in fact utilizing both of the concepts. To sweeten the deal, Frank proposed that they rewrite the chorus to Jackson's current single, *Billie Jean*, to create a jingle for the television advertisements, thereby employing a form of product placement.

The kicker, however, was that in exchange for all of this, Frank wanted triple the amount that Coca-cola had offered, with a partnership for future campaigns that would generate even more. In the end, the deal was signed on the plane before they landed: Enrico and Dileo struck a handshake deal for *more than triple*, a $5 million partnership between Jackson and Pepsi that would obliterate past records for a celebrity endorsement deal, and extricably link Michael Jackson and Pepsi for well over a decade.

The campaign conceived by Dileo and Enrico that night would be the first "integrated marketing campaign" and set the bar for the marketing and endorsement industries for years to come. The rewritten chorus to *Billie Jean* -- "You're the Pepsi generation/Guzzle down and taste the thrill of the day/And feel the Pepsi way" – marked one of the first instances of a hit song being rewritten to include references to the product. Pepsi and Jackson launched the "Next Generation" campaign in multiple channels, traditional print and television advertisements, Jackson logos on the Pepsi packaging, sponsorship posters on Jackson's tours, displays in retail, and a plethora of PR-friendly tie-ins, thus creating one of the original multi-modal campaigns. And, of course, it was rather fortuitous, almost suspiciously so, that Jackson's hair caught fire while making the Pepsi commercial and led to rumors of his first cosmetic surgery. There were speculations as to why Jackson wore sunglasses in the commercial. These exigent circumstances and rumors are often seeds planted by press agents in the fertile soil of the news cycles, creating a "buzz" around the hype. Frank assured me that there was no real truth to these rumors and speculations, but as I said I was never quite sure when Frank was being serious. In this case, fortuitous or intentional, these "mysteries" help insure that the "King of Pop" was going to be everywhere.

Ripples of impact generated by Dileo's deal continue to lap the shores of the entertainment and advertising industries. "...[I]t was definitely game-changing. You couldn't separate the tour from the endorsement from the licensing of the music, and then the integration of the music into the Pepsi fabric," says Brian J. Murphy, EVP of branded entertainment at TBA Global.[60] Pepsi's sales increased to $7.7 billion in 1984 briefly overtaking the real King of Pop, Coca-Cola, a rare occasion.[61] That was enough to land Dileo and Jackson an even better endorsement deal with Pepsi, worth $10 million, after the release of *Bad*, in the late 80's.

This story incorporates all of the ingredients of successful celebrity endorsements and lifestyle branding outlined in this book, but the "take away" here is that Dileo thought outside the box. He did not let the fact that it had never been done before stop him from demanding $3 million dollars for the deal in exchange for services and elements that had never been offered before. In the end, he got $5 million. It is one of those legendary and groundbreaking moments that will forever be studied and talked about.

The beauty of celebrity endorsements is that the landscape of the industry is constantly changing, and the creative ground is fertile for innovators to plant new seeds and create new ideas. Take the ideas in this book and build your own career licensing fame. Draw inspiration from a lyric from the song that give this book its name:

"Take that money and watch it burn
and sink in the river the lessons I've learned."

---

[60] *Ibid.*
[61] *See,* Coke vs. Pepsi: The Cola Wars, CnnTees.com, October 27, 2011.

ABOUT THE AUTHOR

Barry Neil Shrum, Esquire is an entertainment attorney who has been practicing law for over 20 years, representing some of most famous celebrities in the entertainment and creative industries, including everyone's favorite Shark from ABC's *Shark Tank*, Daymond John. Several of his celebrity clients are at the forefront of the licensing industry. Mr. Shrum also teaches copyright, entertainment law, licensing, music publishing and cyberlaw at the prestigious Mike Curb College of Entertainment and Music Business at Nashville's Belmont University. He currently lives in the suburbs of Music City USA (Nashville) where he enjoys spending time with his family.

To have Barry Neil Shrum, Esquire speak at your organization about the principles found in *Counting Stars*, or similar legal concepts and topics , e-mail info@shrumlaw.com. Read Mr. Shrum's first book *Origins of an Idea*, also found on Amazon. Find out more about Mr. Shrum at www.barryshrum.com, or follow Mr. Shrum on Twitter @bshrum.